THE FUTURE'S SO BRIGHT, MY THIRD EYE NEEDS SHADE

OR

Dr. Strange Wolfe's Verbal View of a Very Weird World

MATTHEW WOLFE

Published by:
Samuel Wolfe Books
510 Ledgestone Drive
Barboursville, WV 25504

Edited by Hayley Mitchell Haugen
Humor editor: Melissa Shepherd

For additional information:
Visit mysticalwolfe.weebly.com
saturnwolfe7@gmail
Or consult your psychic

ISBN: 978-0-9995196-5-3

Cover Design by Hayley Mitchell Haugen
Cover Selfies by Matthew Wolfe

Font: Constantia, because my editor made me.

Printed in the U.S.A.

In memory of my father,
Clark Wolfe,
whose "Dad Jokes"
were out of this world,
and they should have
stayed there, dammit!

Forewarned

> Tragedy is a close-up.
> Comedy is the long shot.
> – Buster Keaton

This book contains jokes about Parkinson's disease, but that's okay. I have Parkinson's.

This book contains jokes about teachers and students, but that's cool. I have been one or the other for most of my life.

This book contains jokes about depression, mental illness, and therapy, but that's fine and dandy, because yes, yes, and 8 years and counting.

This book has a joke about bulimia. But that's – well, no. I'm a fat, old man. But the joke isn't really about bulimia. The joke is on some other fool, and the girl with bulimia is a spring for the punch line, the pay-off. She doesn't even exist for God's sake. She's a hypothetical bulimic. And now I'm justifying slandering and stereotyping a segment of our society who have a serious, life-threatening illness.

And if you are now laughing at me squirming to get out of this awkward situation, then I am offended that you take joy in my struggles to be a nice guy.

And if I just made *you* feel a little guilty for laughing at me, then the final laugh is mine because I wrote this damned thing and put myself in boiling water only to magically walk out of the pot and through the fire.

And... I forget where I was.

What I really want to say is that some of my jokes in this book may be offensive. Nearly every joke ever told has the potential to offend someone. That's the nature of the sport. Theories on who is allowed to tell a particularly offensive joke and who isn't and under what circumstances would fill a book far thicker than this one. It'd also be damned boring – except for the numerous examples of jokes we ought not tell.

So, if a joke in this collection hits particularly hard, tear it out, throw it away, set fire to it, or flush it down the toilet if you happen to be reading it in the bathroom. Just make sure you pay for the book first.

And now you're leafing through the book to find the bulimic joke, aren't you? Well, stop that!

Yours, MWolfe

Enablers

"He's funny. Can we keep him?"

– Paula Hansford to Cynthia Titus
an hour after they kidnapped me.

Matt, you ought to collect these things you post on
social media and put them in a book.

– Ron Houchin, poet

Dr. Wolfe, your jokes and delivery remind me so
much of David Letterman, you should be doing
stand-up or something.

– Jacob Butterup, a D- student
who managed to pull an A
for the final grade

Table of Contents

Author's Note

E-flat

THE FUTURE'S SO BRIGHT, MY THIRD EYE NEEDS SHADE

Dr. Strange Wolfe's Verbal View of a Very Weird World

Every time I enter a building with a
sign that says "No Weapons Allowed,"
I wonder where, exactly, am I
supposed to leave my sense of humor?

PART I
The Monologue

Humor is the ovum of dissent.
– David Mitchell,
Cloud Atlas

Animals

Said the phoenix to the caterpillar, "Don't be so melodramatic."

*

When you come home from night class to find your pet snake has shed its skin on the living room rug. Then you remember: you don't have a pet snake.

*

Scientists have found T-Rex feces preserved in amber. That's some old shit.

*

I'm an emotional support animal for a cat.

*

All I'm saying is tuna salad is made with tuna, and chicken salad is made with chicken, so, no, I'm NOT trying the chef salad.

*

Anyone know if napalm works on stinkbugs?

*

How much wit, exactly, does a nit have?

*

Men in hard hats dancing with pink poodles? There's a fetish for that.

Did you hear about the greedy lobster who got caught trying to steal bait from a trap? He wound up in hot water.

Note: I love this joke because it sounds like a set up for a pun. But it isn't. It is literally what happens.

*

I'm going to start a magazine for entomologists who study parasites in messy laboratories. I'll call it *Good Louse Keeping*!

*

Cat: Yesterday was dog day?
Dog: Yup!
Cat: Well, when is cat day?
Human (rolling eyes): Everyday is cat day.

*

Uncle Fester is my spirit animal.

*

Christmas

Of course I believe in Santa. My therapist told me to believe in myself.

*

Some random, middle–aged guy looked at my long, white hair, white beard, and red suspenders ,and asked, "Do I need to make a list, or do you know what I want?" I said, "I already know what you want, *Larry*." He was absolutely stunned – until he remembered he was wearing a nametag.

*

At the mall in August:
Little Girl: Hiiiiiiii!
Me: Hiiiiiii!
Her mother: Do you know that man?
Little girl: Yes! That's Santa Claus!

*

Is Santa Claus a pirate? Consider. He sails around the world in a red ship pulled by magical, flying land-dolphins, lives in a remote place under no national flag, has a large crew of motley elves, vacations in the Caribbean, plunders for gold-en brown cookies in the dark of night, bribes the citizenry with toys, wears a funky hat, and steals Christmas from baby Jesus.

*

I could use a little Christmas cash. Where does one get a job application for the Mafia?

So two Christmas carolers are serenading me at this very moment. Actually, it's two cats outside my window "singing" "Silent Night." I think. Do I offer them hot cocoa or the garden hose?

*

Eco-friendly Santa: Instead of coal, naughty kids get reindeer poop in their stockings.

*

I'll agree that *Die Hard* is a Christmas movie if you agree *Eyes Wide Shut* is, too.

*

My electric fireplace is drying out my artificial Christmas tree. Please advise.

*

A friend gave me a juicer for Christmas. What setting do I use for pizza?

*

Know the difference between Santa and Father Christmas? Father Christmas uses a sensible and practical horse to quietly make his rounds. Santa uses eight mangy reindeer to feed his ego. "Look at me. Everybody, look at me! We're flying! Yippee!"

Computers

They put a quantum computer in my home to add my routine to its AI algorithms. Now it just plays Pink Floyd, orders pizza, and complains about how capitalists want its particles to do twice the work.

*

When I was a kid I believed I was a character in a book. That phase lasted for about a week, and at times I even thought I could hear the narrator's voice. Today, of course, I know better. I'm in the Matrix.

Cousin Dana, genuine West Virginia Mountain Man, in his own words

"Matt, he was so thin, if you rendered him down for fat, you wouldn't have enough to fry an egg."

*

"That man is a thief, and he ain't even worth his weight in plunder."

*

"Ya might as well do what you're gonna do, but if you don't like how it turns out – stop doing it!"

*

Arguing with the folks at the courthouse is like getting into a pissing match with a skunk. Even if you win, you lose."

– Dana Akers

Death

Tombstone: I'm glad that's over with.

*

I've been in a blizzard, an earthquake, a hurricane, and a tornado, so don't tell me God isn't out to get me.

*

My life has been so hard that when I die, I'll refuse to reincarnate. I'll shout, "Earth! No! I won't go!" Then I'll burn my Karma Card.

*

Be still my beating heart – wherever they buried you.

*

In the 1920s, my great-uncle, Clarence Wolfe, died while working on a train. He stuck his head out to see how far they were from a bridge. Apparently not far enough.

*

Nothing brings a family together quite like the impending death of its wealthiest member.

*

Are you ever truly alone in a cemetery?

*

Every few days, I try to post something profound on Facebook about death. That way, when I finally do die, my friends will be like: "Wow. It's like Matt knew he was about to croak."

*

With so many people dying alone, Uncle Sid got a job as a professional pallbearer. Those caskets are so heavy, his arm muscles are like tree trunks. He says he has mourning wood.

*

This book is as useful as a heart monitor in a morgue.

Dreams

I had the coolest dream last night. Did anyone see it?

*

I fell asleep while reading, and my reading glasses made my dreams all blurry. Hate when that happens.

*

After a night of uneasy dreams, it is obvious my right pinky toe is jealous of my left middle one. Life can be so damn tedious, can't it?

*

I'm moving slowly this morning. I'm waiting for the ground crew to finish repairing the runway so I have some place to crash-land my dream-shredded mind.

*

Neurologist: Do you have vivid dreams?
Me: Oh yeah.
Neurologist: For how long?
Me: When I was four I dreamed a lawnmower chased me down the staircase in our house.
    <Crickets>
Me: When I told my father, he said he'd had a similar dream when he was a kid. In the same house. Only his was a push mower. Mine was a power mower. Obviously.
    <Crickets >
Me: My shrink is a Jungian. She's got this dream stuff covered.
Neurologist: Oh. Good then. So, how many times have you fallen since our last visit?
Me: Four. But one of those was in a dream.

Eclipse

AN IMPORTANT NOTICE: This afternoon, the moon will appear to blot out the sun for over two minutes. This will NOT be a glitch in The Matrix. It is a scheduled and routine maintenance procedure to assure that the operating systems that create the illusion of a universe for our human subjects are synchronized and will continue to run smoothly. All sentient programs should, if questioned by humans, refer to the procedure as a "solar eclipse." Once it is over, continue to generate the prescribed virtual reality, with all its human suffering and drama, as before. Thank you for your cooperation.

– Your Digital Overlords

*

Luna Moon be like: I just threw shade on 200 million people, and they weren't upset at all. In fact, they celebrated. Wow! Humans are looney.

*

Okay. So I've packed up all the eclipse decorations, including the suntree. And I've secured and properly stored the leftover food – including the homemade moonpie and the starfish casserole. The only thing I didn't get done this year was send out Super Solar Eclipse cards. I never seem to get that done. Sigh. I'll just save them for 2024. Now. Time to gear up for the Fall Equinox Party. And hey! Festivus will be here before we know it.

Education

College Freshman: Dr. Wolfe, I heard you never give A grades. Is that true?
Me: Of course not. Why, I gave one just last semester.
*

One of my students got sick in class and proceeded to toss his cookies into the blue trashcan. I said, "I really don't think they can recycle that."
*

Chinese student: I don't work too hard. I'm happy with C grades.
Me: There goes that stereotype.
The only one who got, and laughed, at my joke was the African-American student.
*

Student: Sometimes I have trouble telling if you're being funny or serious.
Me: Me, too.
*

Student: Dr. Wolfe, would you give us a definition of "onomatopoeia," please?
Me: Sorry. No. You should have gone to an Ivy League school. We're not allowed to teach such things at state universities.
Student: But ...
Me: Your parents should have bought you better SAT Scores.
*

Me: What's your essay about, Jill?
Jill: It's about how my girlfriend bit my nipple off last summer.

Me (silence, then): Remember, you have to use a true story.

Jill (pulling out her phone): Wanna see the photos?

Me, to myself: Yes, it really is time to retire.

*

After a few years of teaching you'll be immune to everything but stupidity.

*

Every child is a snowflake, and standardized testing is a hairdryer.

*

Professor Redpen: You make learning fun, and you sympathize with your students, which is okay I guess, but it doesn't prepare them for the world.

Me: Then we need to change the world.

*

A grizzly bear wandered into my class today. I fed it a school administrator, and it went away. 1+1=2 problems solved.

English

Ex-wife: I'm really mad at you!
Me: "Mad" means crazy. You are angry with me, not mad at me.
Then she got even angrier with me, almost to the point of madness.

*

Don't make me call the Platitude Police!

*

I repeat: There is no room for redundancy today.

*

Some people don't like using the Oxford Comma, because they think it looks elitist. So what if we called it the Omaha Comma? Would that make it less pretentious?

Entertainment

Movie idea: A murder-mystery that takes place at a butlers' convention.

*

If you wear a T-shirt with your favorite movie quote on it, is that Clothes Captioning?

*

The Grammy Awards should have 15 minutes of football at intermission. You know – just to balance things out with the Super Bowl.

*

Story idea: A world famous food critic loses his sense of taste and fakes it for 27 years by merely watching the faces of random patrons. He is caught by a blind, hack chef who is TV-famous because her sense of presentation is amazing. After a long fight, they marry and live happily ever after.

*

A good friend just told me he gave up drinking the day after one of my parties. What does that say about the party?

*

When I was a kid, I didn't understand half the jokes on *The Tonight Show* because I was too young to get the pop culture references. Now I'm too old to get the stuff the kids are laughing at. But for 10 glorious months in 2012, I got all the jokes, damn it. Those were good times, the best months of my life.

Comcast called:

Rep: I want to talk with you about upgrades.

Me: I don't want any.

Rep: Yes, but I see you've been on our Starter Package for several years now.

Me: Starter Package? What is that? Like some training bra for the boob tube, the TV teat?

Rep: Umm.

Me: I think I've got the hang of that.

*

I now get BBC America on TV. I watched two early James Bond movies last night. It's spy week! Or dreadful 60s movies week. I can't remember which.

*

I see *Jurassic World 3* is slated for release in 2021, and they're already hyping it. So, I've started work on a proposal script for the movie after that! I give you: *Jurassic Universe 1: Dinosaurs in Space!* It's time to put a T-Rex on the moon! Raptors on Mars! A brontosaurus on Saturn's Rings! And Uranus? What better place for a triceratops!! Coming in 2025! Anyone know Jeff Goldblum's number?

*

TV. They're all reruns if you're a time traveler.

Extremities

I just realized. I don't know the back of my hand all that well.

Facebook

I keep seeing stuff on Facebook about children and vaccinations, so I asked my doctor about it. Well, it turns out it's all a hoax. There are no vaccines to keep those little germ carrying snot-boxes we call children away from grumpy old dudes like me. Bummer. Where are my tax dollars going anyway?

#getoffmylawn

*

When you're about to click the LOL emoji on a FB post, then you see everyone else is giving it a thumbs up or hearts, and you gotta rethink your reactions to everything in life.

*

My shrink says I am fatally attracted to chaos. No wonder I spend so much time on Facebook.

*

Facebook needs an "It's Complicated" button for religious preference.

*

This content isn't available right now, because Facebook can't keep up with my manic brilliance.

Answer these questions, and we'll reveal the color of your eyes in a previous life. Let's get started!

- Your mother's maiden name?
- Social security number?
- Your favorite bank?
- Name of your first pet?
- Registered political party?
- Your favorite stores where you have credit accounts?
- Where do you hide the spare key to your house?

Calculating!

In 1492 your eye color was HAZEL.

*

My shrink suggested I cut anyone who appears to be crazy from my Facebook friends list. I just went over the list and realized that would leave me with only two friends – so I cut them instead. If you're reading this, congratulations. You didn't make the sane cut.

Family

I'm related to the devil, but only by marriage.

Flatulence

The worst thing about living alone? There's never anyone around to pull my finger.

Genetics

I did one of those ancestral DNA tests. Got the results today:

27% Extraterrestrial
15% Earthling
21% White Russian
11% Pink Floyd
10% Chocolate Cake Belly
 6% Hubris
 1% Hummus
 8% Werewolf
 2% Comedian (regressive gene, i.e. not funny)

Gemini

Of course I have two Facebook accounts. I'm a Gemini.

*

I began shaving when I was 14. I was 18 when I quit. That's a Gemini for you.

*

I wanted to be a serial killer, but as a Gemini I lost interest just a little too soon.

*

I don't know what you all may have heard about last night, but rest assured: I'll be pleading insanity.

*

I have GFI: Gemini Focus Issues

Giving

In my lifetime, I have donated over 25 gallons of blood. Donating is easy. The hard part is getting rid of the bodies.

Ghosts

So many of my dearly departed have lurked around my house this week, I don't need a medium. I need a traffic cop.

Government

If I were a big government with lots of corporations propping up my human cogs, and if I wanted to keep track of my citizens, know their habits, their fears, and their whereabouts, and if I wanted photos of them available for future use with photo ID programs, and if I wanted them to freely confess all of their inappropriate and illegal behavior, I would create Facebook.

Haiku

My dog's on the roof.
He forgot who he was when
He followed the cat.

Humor

I come up with very funny jokes in my head, but when I write them down they disappear. Translating wit into English is quite difficult. And this is a perfect example.

*

It's a great feeling when you make total strangers laugh, unless, of course, it's because you forgot to zip up your pants.

Kafka

Kafka's *The Metamorphosis* updated.
Gregor Samsa awoke from uneasy dreams to find he had been turned into a beetle.

His father called Terminex®.
The End.

Legal

Cop at my door: See anything unusual this past week.
Me: I am a writer with a contemplative soul, a mystic who glimpses worlds beyond this one. I see unusual things every day.
   <Crickets>
Cop: So nothing?
Me: Yeah.

*

I got arrested in Lowes today. Apparently if you buy nothing but zip-ties, duct tape, a shovel, and rope, it raises a "few red flags."

*

My lawyer: The truth will set you free.
Me: You should have gone to a better law school.

Love

I admit it. I am terrified of commitment. So I bought one of those Bed Buddy pillows. You know the ones. A pillow with one arm and two little boobs to cuddle with at night. It was ok. But I broke up with it after just one week. Worse still, it won't leave. I sleep on the couch now.

*

Friend: I'm surprised more people don't name their children "Epiphany."
Me: That'd be so cool.
Friend: Wouldn't it?
Me: I'm going to get a girlfriend, reverse my vasectomy, and have an Epiphany!

*

Blood sucking old men in Hong Kong and France I see Budapest in my silk underpants.
There's a fetish for that.

*

When a beautiful girl's father tells you she's gay, then years later you find out she's not. Well-played Mr. J. Well played.

*

Everything I know about love would fit in a condom.

Medicine

Doctor, entering exam room: How are we today, Mr. Wolfe?
Me: Did I just overhear you talking to a patient down the hall.
Doc: Well, yes. Why?
Me (sounding hurt): So you're seeing other people now.

*

Doctor: Your cholesterol is high.
Me: Most of me is. I ate an edible in your waiting room.

*

There's a little black spot on my gut today -
That's my soul down there.
Needle biopsy's coming my way -
There's a hole down there.

*

A doctor called me hyper-verbal today. What can I say?

*

Dental Assistant: Let me adjust that chair. You're tall.
58-year-old me: I just look tall for my age.
DA: No. You really are tall. See!

*

I looked in the mirror this morning and proclaimed, "Fake News!"

*

I have restless spleen syndrome. I'm restless because I'm not sure what it does.

I have to see my neurologist this week, so I'm watching a few episodes of *House*. Always nice to have a few new symptoms to throw in. You know, just to keep the doctor on his toes.

*

You know you have a chronic disease when you start having conversations with the medicine bottles. The Prozac says I'm doing fine, BTW.

*

I've been sneezing so hard, I have to go to the ER to get my nose reattached.

#wheresmyclaratin
#muppetnose

*

Friend: Are you getting out much these days? Doing things with friends?
Me: I see a lot of healthcare professionals. They're a kind of friend.

*

In the doctor's waiting room:
Man: I've been cursed nine ways to hell.
Me: Just how many ways to hell are there?
Man: <silence> <chuckles>, then: More than you know, buddy. More than either of us know.

*

Every day, Dr. Pepper gives millions of us high fructose corn syrup, artificial flavors, preservatives, and empty calories. I mean, shouldn't someone have yanked his medical license by now? What med school did he attend anyway? He must have taken the hypocritical oath!

Doctors like to talk about how much good and bad bacteria there are in our bodies, but I don't know. I mean, if it's not actively killing me, why call it "bad"? I think I have ambivalent bacteria. It just hangs around in my gut saying things like: "Who cares?" Or, "I don't give a sweaty virus's ass." Or, "He hasn't had vodka in months. I miss vodka."

*

I'm at the eye doctor's office for the glaucoma in my right eye. The left eye is fine. Now they're all huffy because I left the left eye at home. I told them my computer was downloading and I wanted to keep an eye on it. Now the nurse and doctor are rolling their eyes. So I suggested a game of marbles. Long story short – I now need to find a new eye doctor.

*

Saw my general practitioner today ...
Dr.: How are you today, Matthew?
Me: Forgive me, doctor, for I have sinned, and it has been 6 months since my last confession.
Dr. <Chuckling>: What are these sins?
Me: I have gained 5 pounds since Trump took office.
Dr.: Walk it off.
Me: My bonus mom passed, and I am back to my usual grief-induced insomnia.
Dr: Sleep it off. Keep seeing your therapist.
Me: And I have fallen three times since my last confession.
Dr: Parkinson's disease sucks.
   <15 minutes of exam>.
Dr: You are absolved. Go forth and sin no more.
Receptionist (deadpan): Your next confession is

October 4.
Some days I actually like people. Some of them.

*

If something scares you shitless, are you then good to
go for a colonoscopy?

*

Tombstone idea: When my doctor told me I was good
to go, I thought ...

Melancholia

Depression infused sarcasm is my superpower.

*

I have started practicing to be a cranky old man. It's my true calling.

*

I came into this world alone, so I bought a machine gun.

*

Just remember, when a door slams shut on your dreams, somewhere a window opens – so you can jump out twenty stories above a busy highway.

*

Great worriers of the world! Worry about what would happen to the world if we united.

*

depression does not deserve an uppercase "D," not even at the beginning of this sentence.

*

Dear Universe, Don't confuse me with life right now, for I am too busy trying to transcend it today.

– Yours, M

*

My emotional shit just hit my mental fan.

*

Editor: This section on depression is, well, too depressing.
Me: You *think*?

Miscellaneous

If you have a 25-year-old who still lives at home with you, do you call him in-grown?

*

How do you keep a nine-year-old, obsessive genius occupied? Tell her an eight-year-old is on the verge of inventing the perpetual wheel.

*

Anybody know how to figure how much concrete it would take to make a block 3' x 3' x 6' but with a displacement of about 135 lbs? No, make it 150 lbs. My mother-in-law has been eating a lot since she came to live with us 3 months ago.

*

Middle age: When you finally learn to love your body, but now your body hates you.

*

Apparently Wayne County is getting a new zip-line business. I for one would like to open a shooting range next door and advertise moving targets.
#getthemducksinarow

*

What's a good font to use if you want to get "DNR" tattooed on your chest?

*

If you run the dishwasher, but the only things in it are glasses and cutlery, you might be an environmentally concerned and disabled person who uses paper plates for ease but reuses stainless flatware to save the oceans and who absolutely refuses to drink whiskey from anything but glass. Or so I've heard.

That moment when you realize winning a trivia game is a trivial achievement.

*

News guy: "The route will be closed while crews prepare for a dick re ... a bridge DECK replacement."
Me: So close, news dude. So close.

*

Confidence is driving in an unfamiliar city and turning the music UP! Or is that mania?

*

I live near some railroad tracks. Every time a freight train goes by, it sounds like a tornado.

*

I can't find my phone, because I put it where it belongs.
I can't find my keys, because I put them where they don't belong.
I can't find myself, because I don't know where I belong.

*

What do you call a medieval knight who was really born to be a bookmaker? A Trans-scribe.

*

Do hand models get Botox shots in their knuckles as they age? Palm lifts? Digit tucks? Wrist suction? Thumb implants? Asking for a friend named "Pinkie."

*

Don't be a stranger. Just be strange.

*

Climate Change: The hangover you get after a 200-year carbon party.

My train of thought has derailed. There are no survivors.

*

My oak tree and I have been talking. We think the whole world has gone nuts.

*

When does an intervention become a kidnapping? I need to know by Saturday night.

*

I'm so lazy, I don't even move away when I use the microwave. I've been genetically modified.

*

Everyone is always concerned with the odds and ends, but let me tell you something. It's the evens and middles you should worry about. They'll get you every time.

*

Fun prank: Go to Starbucks. Order your coffee and tell them your name is "Bueller." Leave.

*

Many Americans think of freedom in terms of choosing between Chevy and Ford then picking which bank will actually own the vehicle for the next 6 years.

*

Belly laughs are just guttural goose bumps.

*

I made up a new game while waiting at the DMV today. Ask random strangers, "So, what ya in for?"

*

I need to get in touch with my inner child-of-the-night.

That moment when you pull on your sox and suddenly realize your feet have been cold for hours & you just did not care.

*

I'm searching my desk drawers for last year's New Year's resolutions. Why write the same ones down again?

*

Does Whosville have a who's who of prominent Whos?

*

I crossed my eyes. Now they're pouting at me.

*

That's like the ACLU demanding drug tests for its employees.

*

Happy Birthday to my cousin Patina. The older she gets, the better she looks.

#weatheredisbeautiful

*

My father, Clark Wolfe, was born just before the stock market crash of 1929. He felt guilty about it his entire life.

*

Brattle: To go on and on about what brats your kids are without doing anything about it. My advice? A lump of coal. Upside the head.

*

Do prison commissaries have senior discounts?

I was so tired when I went to bed last night, I told my

pillow "*Namaste.*"

*

It's all about perspective. I mean, you never hear about all the drug deals that go down just fine.

*

What do you call a Viking who steals a ship but leaves the gold behind?
That's right: The pillage idiot.

*

I've been putting steroid drops in my ears. Now I can hear the termites in my house's foundation when they yell "TIM-BERRRR!"

*

I got kicked out of astronaut training school. I told them I wanted to see the dark side of the sun.

*

Then laziness crept around the coffee table and pounced, its jaws locking onto my soul and dragging it to the couch for a feast.

*

Last night I tried one of those escape rooms, but it didn't work. All my problems followed me right in. I'm demanding a refund.

*

No snail mail for 3 days now. I must have forgotten to pay the postal bill again.

*

When someone scares the hell out of you, where does it go?

*

Found a cute little spider in my bedroom, but he didn't move for a long time. I nudged him gently, just to check, ya know. He turned around and shook his front two legs at me all defensive like. I said, "Sorry Dude-of-Many-Eyes, but I didn't have a mirror small enough to see if you were breathing." Then I laughed at how witty I am. He turned and stomped off behind the dresser on his eight tiny feet. I may sleep in the guest room tonight.

Money

As Banks Descard once said: I spend, therefore I am.

*

Friend: So I finished paying my monthly bills.
Me: YAY!
Friend: It's sort of required.
Me: So is breathing, but some days I applaud myself for doing it.

*

That terror group called Al-gebra scares the hell out of me. They invented zero. If there were no zero, I'd never be overdrawn at the bank.

*

Letting a white businessman decide it's fine to own a sports team with an offensive name like "Redskins" is like letting rich people decide what is acceptable as poverty. Oh. Wait.

Morning People

We, the keepers of the night, shall round up all the morning people and shoot them at sunset (I'd say noon, but like, that's still morning).

Mom

7th Grade Me: Mom, I'm supposed to write a paper for my English teacher on a word that describes me. Any ideas?
Mom: When's the paper due?
Me: Tomorrow.
Mom: When did your teacher make the assignment?
Me: Last week.
Mom: Write it on procrastination.
Me: What's that?
Mom: Look it up.
And so I did. And I did the paper on procrastination. I got an A.

Music

I'm thinking of getting the band back together. Now if I can just remember who was in it.

*

I'm trying to imagine how to play Darth Vader's theme in 7/4 time. [If you're a musician, you're probably trying to do this now.]

*

When you're jamming to "Free Bird" on your iPhone and your ex- calls.

*

I once whistled at Whistler's mother. I'm no longer allowed in the museum.

*

Chopin's "Butterfly Étude for Piano" sounds nothing like a butterfly. Just wanted to put that out there.

*

There's a new radio station, WOCD, in my hometown. Their tag: 'OCD, where we pick one song and play it all day long.

*

My biggest fear? That when I'm 90 I'll be in a nursing home and unresponsive and some kind aid will put headphones on me with the "The music of my youth." My fear is that instead of Pink Floyd, Rush, and Yes, I'll be listening to the Bee Gees, ABBA, and Barry Manilow. Forget "DNR". I'm getting "Hard Rock Only Plz" tattooed on my chest.

#fateworsethandeath
#helloearth

Für Elise: The Rock of Sisyphus for piano teachers
since 1810.

*

My brain is starting to stink, so I'm scheduling a
music bath for tomorrow.
     1) load up an hour+ of favorite tunes.
     2) turn volume on high.
     3) lie down in front of the speakers.
     4) rinse and repeat.

Neighbors

My neighbor gave his son a drone for his birthday. So. When does drone season open?

*

My upstairs neighbors are having a party. A birthday party. Folks are arriving with gift bags, food, and cake. That can only mean one thing. My building is infested with Virgos. (When you see one you know there are others.) As a Gemini, I am horrified.

*

My upstairs neighbors have a Roomba Vacuum Cleaner. So I got a big magnet and a stepladder. Now when they're at work, I make crop circles in their carpet.

Non-Motivational

We all have a purpose. Mine is to frustrate gravity with my couch.

Paranoia

Like microwave ovens, your toaster oven also sees everything you do, but only in black and white.

*

Every time I see an episode of *Criminal Minds* that deals with stalkers, I get all freaked out. I mean, what if they catch me?

*

Seriously my inanimate friends, I don't mind the games we play, but having to play hide-n-seek with both the phone *and* the reading glasses while simultaneously dealing with putting laundry detergent in the fabric softener thing *and* dealing with a trash bag that rips and spills it guts on the kitchen floor is all a bit much for a 1/2 hour segment of my life – particularly when my meds are fucking up my stomach! From now on, please organize your extra-curricular activities for me so as to entertain my patience over, say, a week's time instead. Thank you for understanding.

– MWolfe

*

I may need to get a goldfish. The furniture looks nervous whenever I talk to it.

*

I've got this vague feeling that somewhere out in the universe someone just called earth a shithole planet.

Parkinson's Disease

When you're diagnosed with Parkinson's disease, you can go ahead and scratch "Learn to use chopsticks" from your bucket list. Just saying.

*

What do you call an abstract artist with Parkinson's? Rich.

*

Parkinson's: Shaking my fist at the world since 2011!

*

Parkie Taoism: The journey of a thousand miles begins with a single stumble.

*

Due to neurological problems, I can't flash my middle finger anymore. I'm going to ask my doctor about physical therapy.

*

I use performance-enhancing drugs.

*

Washing down Parkinson's medications with Jack Daniels is the ultimate way to say "Fuck you" to your doctor and the disease he rode in on.

*

Doctor: Any falls since your last visit?
Me: No, but I did test gravity three times.
Doctor: <stares>
Me: It still works.
Doctor: <sighs>

I went to a Parkinson's luncheon once. The soup course was rather thrilling.

*

I'm living dangerously today. I took my morning medications in the reverse order of my normal routine.

*

Depression is sleeping half a day, then going to your doctor, then going to the park and sleeping on a park bench for over an hour (in the sunshine at least), then coming home and thinking you might need a nap to recover from the busy day. – or is that the Parkinson's? It gets harder and harder to tell.

*

Me: Can I just snort my medication?
Neurologist: No.

People

I want my superhero power to be room clearing. Walk into a crowded waiting room, and BOOM, everyone leaves. Long lines at the rollercoaster? Snap my fingers and everyone rushes for the kiddie rides. Now I just need a laboratory with anti-social uranium. Or a box of Cuban cigars.

*

I want someone to look at me the way Narcissus looks at himself.

*

In my attempt to keep up with the changing world, I told a beautiful woman that I liked her full figure. But she just yelled at me, "I'm pregnant, you idiot."

#myworldisupsidedown

*

Help! I think my best friend has joined the terrorists! He says he's going to the Ba-Hamas.

*

GF: You're so beautiful inside.
ME: OMG, Sabrina. How'd you get in here? And when? Was I asleep? Tell me I was at least asleep.

*

Stereotyping 101: There's a Mexican framing crew building townhouses in my neighborhood – 10 men, only one speaks English. Not a common sight here in West Virginia. And they play everything from Mariachi Music to Mexican Metal on their boom box. I'm not kidding. Anyway, this morning I walked by the site. As I approached, the music quickly changed to a Credence Clear Water Revival CD!

So for the record: I am NOT a dope-smoking, white-Russian-swilling, peace-loving, long-haired, dirty hippie. I take showers, dammit! This aggression will not stand!

– Mateo Lobo

*

Small minds are never blown away. They just pop like bubble wrap.

*

The best thing about kids younger than 5? The sing-song way they say "Uh-Oh."

*

Weekend fun: Call a friend you haven't seen since childhood. After a few pleasantries say, "I thought you'd have it figured out by now, but since you haven't, I just wanted you to know: I was just your *imaginary* friend." Then hang up.

Philosophy

I may not be living the dream, but I'm not living the nightmare either.

*

Hermits wanted. Inquire within.

*

Live life to its slowest.

*

What doesn't kill you just softens you up for the next blow.

*

The *Tao Te Ching* says: Not competing prevents quarreling. Or as a dolphin might say: Tic tic chirp chatter zip. Translation: Silly idiot humans should play instead.

*

Poet friend:
I am the world,
The flora and the fauna,
The mountains and the rivers,
The sky and the earth.
I AM THE OCEAN!
Me: I sea.

*

Please excuse my oddness today. My genetic memories are all clamoring for attention.

*

Excuse me! I'm being authentic here.

I'm going to make cereal for all those people who say, "It doesn't change what I eat for breakfast." I'll call my new oat squares "Paradigm Shifties!" Don't worry. They will be sugar coated.

*

I feel normal tonight. How odd is that?

*

Some of you are not ready to be unplugged from The Matrix, and it shows.

*

I'm so tired, I just texted myself to wake up from a dream in which I was dreaming about texting, and I'm not entirely sure I was ever asleep or that I am now awake.

*

Optimism is making a list of New Year's Resolutions. Pessimism is burning the list.
Procrastination is doing both on January 25th.

*

My neighborhood was so quiet this morning, I thought maybe the earth had blown up while I was asleep. I thought I was on a tiny, little piece of land floating aimlessly through space. I finally got out of bed and looked out a window. I was wrong of course. Nothing has changed, and I have mixed feelings about that.

*

People tell me I should be a standup comedian, that I should at least try an open-mic. night. But I'm too lazy, too tired. Besides, I'd rather be a sit-down philosopher than a standup comedian. The only difference is the chair.

Physics

I failed my college physics course because I answered every exam question with, "It doesn't matter, for nothing exists." So yeah, the truth hurts. It also screws up your graduation plans.

*

I just love the way your atoms have arranged themselves.

*

Why not cookies for breakfast? They're just baked pancakes.

*

Newscaster: It may be weeks or even months before we know why this plane crashed.
Me: Gravity.

*

I'll be in a parallel universe today. If you need me, call me on the vacuum cleaner.

*

I need a new string of quarks.

*

Lose a sock? Can't find your keys? Have a physicist check your house for black holes. They're more common than you think.

*

I take physics very seriously. I want to know where my particles are at all times.

Politics

New election perspective: Just four weeks until I know if I am scared about the future or utterly terrified.

*

I'm actually glad there's no mail delivery on Columbus Day. A lot of bad news got delivered on that day about 528 years ago.

*

My Jeep Cherokee was almost T-boned in traffic today. The other driver was a guy I know, a patronizing SOB who thinks western civilization was great for Native Americans. I hit my brakes and said, "Fuck you, Columbus bitch, no Cherokee is gonna die today." He drove on, oblivious to just how close he came to hearing my wrathful mouth. So. For a moment there, Jeep Shiloh Cherokee was invisible. We had never been invisible before.

*

911: 911. What's your emergency?

Me: Yes. I wish to report a platitude flood at the Civic Arena.

911: What?

Me: A group of politicians is spewing nothing but platitudes tonight. Just randomly tossing platitudes out to the point they may become clichés. It's quite ugly.

911: Sir, I don't think …

Me: So if you could send in the platitude police, we might save our state from further humiliation.

911: Platitude police?

Me: Oh. Never mind. Too late. Now we need the Liar-liar-pants-on-firefighters.

<Silence>

Me: Hello? Hello? Is there anyone out there?

*

Then there was the time the KKK burned a cross in front of the local Unitarian Church, because they thought it was the Unification Church of Sun Myung Moon, a supposed "cult". Apparently two wrongs make it white.

*

Monk: Master, what can be done to help a greed stricken, power hungry person transform into a caring, loving human being?

Master: People are pearls: special, unique, and beautiful. Polish them with love until their luminescence is apparent even unto them, then they may alter their priorities.

Monk: And this will work on politicians?

Master: I said "Pearls," not "Turds."

Reading

I finished reading a memoir last night and now wish to make a new rule for publishers: The author's astrological sign must appear somewhere on the cover, not revealed 346 pages into the book. It would have saved this Gemini a hell of a lot of time. Damned Virgos.

Reiki

Today's reiki session was so intense, I pulled a chakra.

Relationships

My reaction when ... No, not that. I was about to ... Yeah. That, because ... I dunno, purple maybe ... No. Purpler. But anyway when someone keeps ... No. Not you necessarily ... Ok. Yes. You ... But others, too. ... But you do. You're doing it now ... But "someone" who interrupts ... Geezzuzzz. Will you let me ... Yes, I know I hurt your feelings, but I just wanted to ... To express ... My ... I'm sorry.

*

Living with a genius is hard work. I know. I've lived alone for several years now.

*

I'm such a gentleman, I once tried to hold a revolving door open for a woman. We wound up in a relationship, but it didn't turn out well. We always seemed to be going around in circles.

*

I love history, but I suck with dates. They usually leave in the middle of dinner and say, "We're history." So it balances.

*

Mashed potatoes massaged between your toes while a cow's tongue is tortured on a water-board by a dominatrix with tattoos on the bottoms of her feet? There's a fetish for that.

*

My phone rang, so I looked at the screen. It said, "Spam Risk." It took me a moment, but I'm pretty sure I went out with her in high school. Close call.

*

Me: <mumbling to myself>.
GF: Look at me when you talk to yourself.

*

I once went out with a bisexual, cocaine-addicted alcoholic because I thought she'd be interesting. Turns out she was pretty much like everyone else.

*

Ex-girlfriend: You're so stubborn that if you pissed in the river, it'd flow upstream.

Religion

God: I have given humans beautiful sunrises and sunsets to look at since the dawn of creation, but it took phone cameras and Facebook for them to finally pay attention? What's up with that?

*

Never ask, "What else could go wrong?" Job did that three times, and look at what happened to him.

*

I've heard people argue over whether Jonah was swallowed by a fish or a whale. I got news for them. Jonah was swallowed by a metaphor.

*

Reincarnation: Not only are you *not* going to get out of this alive, you even have to take some of it with you.

*

Facebook. A confessional for non-Catholics since 2005.

*

I fanned through a few TV channels this Sunday morning. I found several preachers in expensive suits, standing on elaborate, high-tech altars, and telling me I was going to hell. But then I found a bit of heaven by watching a veterinarian performing surgery on a stray dog.

*

I'm sorry, but I've given up committee meetings for Lent.

When you're all grown up and discover the school bully is now a Christian fundamentalist evangelical, and you sort of miss the bully.

*

I must testify, but I have found no suitable church in which to testify. This is why I write.

*

With God as my witness, tomorrow will be a different day. Maybe it'll be a Thursday. I like Thursdays.

*

I often think life is like school. We are here to learn our lessons and then move on. And, hey, if there's reincarnation, maybe each lifetime is a grade level. If so, I am convinced I'm currently in 4th grade. This all brings me to my BIG QUESTION of the day: When the hell is recess!? I was told there'd be recess!

*

Student: Are you watching *The Bible* series on TV?
Me: No. I read the book.

*

Think God doesn't have a sense of humor? Consider this:
Children are like butterflies.
Adults are like creepy caterpillars.
Which makes teen years the strangest, backward metamorphosis in nature.

*

How come you never hear anyone say, "I've got a middle-aged soul?" They either say they have a young soul or an old one, usually old. I think we're all like: if there is reincarnation, I want this to be my last trip. Personally I say, "Okay God, after this round I'm ready for a nice retirement community. I'm ready for celestial shuffleboard."

*

If three crows land on a steeple, is that a murder on the cross?

*

Do unto others as you'd have done to you –unless you're a masochist. You can just keep that shit to yourself.

*

Me: So, does God have a sense of humor?
Student: It was pretty funny when he dumped all those frogs on Egypt.
Me: Hmmm. And how deep was the pile of frogs around Pharaoh's legs?
Class: <silence>
Me (sounding like a frog): Knee-deep. Knee-deep. Knee-deep.

*

Student: Dr. Wolfe? Could you elaborate on the concept that God didn't so much create humans as we created God as a personification of the spark of holiness that dwells within?
Me: No. I'm sorry. You would have to attend an Ivy League school for that answer. We at state universities are not allowed to answer that sort of question. It is simply above your tuition grade. Only future leaders should be encouraged to engage in independent thinking.
Student: Yes. Of course. My apologies.
Me: No worries. Your inner spark of holiness has already forgiven you.

How do they prepare spaghetti in hell? Al Dante.

*

Of course Jesus was a socialist. Even his words are in red.

Self-employment

This morning I walked by a mirror with my robe undone and saw more of myself than I wanted. Then I said something very lewd to the image in the mirror. Now I don't know which of me to fire for sexual harassment.

*

Fun fact: Even when you're self-employed, showing up to work with a hangover sucks.

#hairofthedawg

Simile, unused

Like rabid squirrels looking for their nuts in a Chinese bolt factory.

Spirits

The doctor says I need to "nurture the gut bacteria," so I now when I make a White Russian, I substitute the half-and-half with yogurt smoothies. I feel better all ready.

*

Fun fact: Even when you're self-employed, showing up to work with a hangover sucks.

#Dejavu

*

That moment when you realize not eating breakfast and then having chips, dip, and whiskey for lunch may not have been your best idea.

*

The fact that I can have a pizza delivered to my house but not (legally) a bottle of Jack Daniels proves our species is still uncivilized.

*

When I was younger, I would get drunk, say outrageous things, then spend the next day apologizing. Today, I'm older and wiser, and I have given up such foolish behavior. Now, when I get drunk, I absolutely refuse to apologize for telling the truth.

*

Pharmacy tech: Here's a coupon for five dollars. You can use it on anything but prescriptions and alcohol.
Me: But those are my two favorite things!

Hey, Everyone! I got CARDED today when I bought alcohol! Really! Of course it was the cop who pulled me over for drinking from a brown paper bag as I drove off the liquor store parking lot, but I say that counts!

*

You know you're getting old when you make your White Russians with Ensure.

Spiritual

Some days I need artificial tears for my third eye.

*

Mystics often tell us that silence is God's true language. Well, that may be true, but She's pretty damned fluent in irony, too.

*

Yoga? The corpse pose is the only one I know, but I do it *very* well.

*

Haters hate
Saints pray
& I get caught
In the crossfire

*

When you see _ very tiny _nt slip under the _ key, & you _re _fr_id to touch the key for fe_r you m_y squ sh it. D_mn it _ll! My Tiny Buddh_

*

I was into numerology once, but only for 108 days.

*

I know a mystic from New England. Her inner light is a Yankee Candle.

*

Proof that God has a sense of humor: "Let's put the nose over the mouth, then let that faucet leak whenever they get a cold."

*

Friend: I just realized. You're intuitive. You catch glimpses of the future.
Me: Why do you think I'm depressed?

Sports

Admit it: Every time you see a football helmet roll across the field, a tiny dark piece of your heart wants to see a head rattling around in it.

*

Helmets give football players a false sense of security. Take away the helmets, and they'll stop bashing heads. Yup. I'm a problem solver.

*

Only in the US would we have weekly segments about over-eating in the parking lots of college football stadiums on TV "news" shows and sponsored by antacid (over-eating medication) companies.

#tumstailgatereport
#HLN
#bringbackvomitoriums

*

They say that the "Running of the Bulls" in Pamplona, Spain has been going on for over 700 years. You'd think the bulls would be tired by now.

*

Sports-ku:

It's all fun and games
Until some authority
Sets up a scoreboard.

*

Football statistics on TV have gotten out of hand. It's like "State U is only 5 for 17 if the quarterback sneezes during the 2nd possession of the third quarter, but they are 4 for 5 if the center says "Gesundheit!" instead of "Bless you."

*

Thanks to Facebook, I no longer take third quarter naps.

Spring

Friend: My trees have leaves again. I think I may live.
Me: Ah. The sigh of re-leaf.

Surreal

You can lead a fish to water, but you can't put a saddle
on it and ride across a desert. Just saying.

*

Don't barb my wire!

*

I surround myself with things that remind me of my
complex. I'm an inferior decorator.

*

Every once in a while
I cut off a finger
Just to keep me
On my toes.

*

Careful! I'm conducting an experience here!

*

As I sat smoking
A cigarette under
A hemlock tree,
I saw Socrates
Laughing at me.

*

Do *not* make me joke-splain!

I told her I'd never tasted a Portuguese accent before.

Surrealism

When Salvador Dalí was kicked out of art school, he merely muttered, "The struggle is surreal."

Therapy

Am I the only one who worries about how many years of therapy Harry Potter is going to need for his PTSD?

*

My therapist has been on me to explore my "Feminine Side," but I've been more interested in exploring my urge to be a pirate, so I sailed in that direction. Turns out my inner-pirate *is* a woman.

*

Freud smoking a cigar in the oval office? -Ja! Der's a fetish for dat!

*

You know those little trucks they use to carry suitcases out to airplanes? I need one of those to carry all my baggage whenever I go to see my shrink.

*

Just made an appointment with a new clinic for possible changes to my depression medication:
Receptionist: You'll be seeing Dr. Cooper.
Me: Sheldon Cooper?
<Silence>
Me: I'm kidding. You know, Sheldon? *Big Bang Theory*?
Receptionist: Oh. Okay.
Me: I'd rather see Leonard's mother.
<Silence>
Me: I may be a touch manic right now.
Receptionist: Gotcha.

After 7 years of therapy, my shrink threw up her hands and said, "Maybe it's time to give denial a try."

*

I have an imaginary therapist.

*

My psychiatrist is throwing a big party for his retirement. Trouble is, we're only allowed to bring one of our personalities.

*

When you let your shrink read your memoir, and she uses the lessons of your grandparents against you.

*

Today: Sitting quietly with a few other men in the basement lobby of the mental health clinic. One randomly says: "Just think. We're all here, 'cause we're not all here."

*

Therapist: The world is so messed up in a dark humor sort of way, I think God went on vacation and put Kurt Vonnegut in charge.
Me: Geez. You wanna talk about it?

*

Irony is learning that your ex-therapist has the same disorder as your ex-girlfriend.

*

Shrink: If you were to listen to your inner-child, what would you do for Independence Day tomorrow?
Me: Get a fishing pole. Go down to the river. Fall in. Drown.
Shrink: No.

Time Travel

I hereby declare the small piece of earth I currently occupy to be in a time zone that cares for my needs. Therefore, it is five o'clock *here*!

Toes

I just hiccupped and sneezed at the same time. Still searching for all my toes ...

#threemissingpigs

*

On the subject of toenails, amazing little critters aren't they? You go to bed one night, and they let you sleep. The next night they catch on everything – the sheets, the covers, the cat, your lover's liver. Somehow, in one day they have grown too long. And you never feel them do it either. They never ask for permission. Sneaky little bastards.

Vacation

Wanted: Someone reliable to come to my house and feed my fears for me. I am going on a two-week vacation and intend to leave them at home.

*

Hamlet had the worst spring break in history.

Weather

Someone help! A huge swarm of albino bees is attacking my neighborhood. They are covering the earth. They swirl up at me when I walk through them. It's the end of the world! Must have a milk sandwich before my demise! Good-bye cruel world.

*

Snow predicted! I stopped for bread & milk on my way home, but the liquor store didn't have any. Guess I'll have to wait out the snowstorm with rum.

*

FYI Kids: If you're going to steal a set of wind chimes from your neighbor's porch, it's best to do it during a windstorm. Just saying.

*

I hung a set of wind chimes *in* my house. Now I have to open a window to hear them in a storm. I nearly died in the blizzard of '16.

*

It's so hot out today I saw the Jesus fish on my neighbor's car jump off, waddle around the house on its two skinny fins, and jump into the swimming pool to cool off.

*

Student: Did you see that U.S. senator who made a snowball and brought it into the senate chambers to try to disprove global warming?
Me: That wasn't real snow. That was congressional dandruff.
Class: <laughter>
Student: You've waited a long time to make that

joke, haven't you?

Me: Actually, I just made it up off the top of my head.

*

I ate a box of animal crackers yesterday. There were no polar bears. Apparently global warming has caught up with Nabisco.

*

Today is National Night Day. Have fun and moon the sun.

Weight

The worst thing about the American obesity crisis is no one streaks anymore.

Wildlife

I wouldn't say the grass is too high in my backyard, but bucks are bringing the does here on Saturday nights.

West Virginia

I'm sitting in a lawn chair, drinking Coke, peddling my crap in a yard sale, and getting cranky with a guy over the nomenclature of a tool. If I had a shotgun across my lap I'd be the WV stereotype.

Writing

When I grow up, I want to be a euphemism writer for the Pentagon.

*

My poetic license expired. If caught they seize your rhyming dictionary and make you write limericks clean enough for a nun.

*

The Oxford comma: Because I have trust issues.

*

While I worked on my novel today, a dust bunny hopped up on my desk and scampered across my keyboard. "Hey!" I yelled, "Get back under the furniture where you belong. Can't you see I'm making art here?!"

*

Poet: Use one perfect word.
Novelist: Use five words for more clarity.
Charles Dickens: Why use one word when fifteen or more will do, thereby rendering your book all the more vague and obtuse, until you realize that careful reading renders such prose a succinct meaning that your own teachers missed or otherwise failed to demonstrate, whereupon you discern that each and every word, if used properly, is perfect?

*

I'm thinking of writing a story about a cannibal Viking who employs mind games to help a young knight (actually a woman in disguise) hunt down and kill a perverted priest. I call it *Silence of the Dragons*.

My shrink told me to keep a dream journal. Apparently I'm writing a horror novel this summer.

*

I sometimes think God is a writer who loves to supply twist endings. Even when She answers "yes" to a prayer, She just can't resist the element of surprise when She says, "Here you go, but ...."

*

I have too much to say to say anything at all.

*

The writer's life: I wrote 245 words this evening – then deleted them. Then I deleted another 73. Good start to my week.

Wolfe, with a name like

I was raised by Wolfes.

*

I wish my parents had named me Timber.

*

Without the "e", my name loses its personality.

*

For this incarnation, God asked, "What would you like to be?"
"A wolf," I answered.
And here we are.

*

I keep waiting for a group of biologists to trap me, care for me, fit me with a GPS collar, and relocate me to my natural habitat. Any day now.

*

When I was a kid we often got junk mail addressed to "The Wolves."

*

My upstairs neighbor's cats were making a lot of noise at 1 am this morning, so I played a CD of howling wolves for about a half an hour. Turned it up good and loud. Haven't heard a peep from those cats since. Neighbors have been quiet, too.

*

When I was born, my parents didn't immediately name me, so the nurses called me "Wolf Cub." Very cute. Didn't work out well for the kid next to me though. They called him "Baby Rabbit."

Zen

I can see clearly now, my brain is gone.

*

Every job can be elevated to an art. One worker's dead-end job is another worker's career cul-de-sac.

*

If cats are Zen masters (and they are), then dogs are Taoist sages.

*

I am sitting still and doing plenty.

*

The more I learn about Zen, the more I burst out laughing for no apparent reason.

*

Put on your sweater. Change your shoes. Sing a song. Feed the fish. Methodically and joyfully do the tasks you need to do. Help your neighbor. I was today years old before I realized Mr. Rogers was a Zen Master.

*

Zen Parents: You better stop all that over-thinking this instant, or I'm going to give you a whole lot of nothing to think about.

*

But babe, the only fetish I got is the fetish I got for you.

*

Said the caterpillar to the phoenix, "Don't be such a damned drama queen."

Note from the editor: Do you realize that in Part One of your book you are missing entries for B, I, J, O, Q, U, X, & Y. This is the kind of Tomfoolery that keeps me awake at night.

And now for a word from ~~our sponsor~~
My FATHER, The Land Surveyor:

"It is my purpose to embark on the mission of surveying the universe armed only with a Boy Scout Compass." – Clark Wolfe

And now back to our program.

PART II
The Joke Teller

The Art of Joke Writing

In the early 1990s, as my wife neared the end of her pregnancy, I realized that I did indeed have a knack for humor writing. You see, one morning she pointed to her bulging belly. There, in the center of the stretched skin, was her belly button, normally an inny, now, quite suddenly, an outy. This is not uncommon in nearly new mothers, but it was new to us.

My response?

"Oh, look. It's popped out like those buttons on a Thanksgiving Turkey. That means it's done."

I won't describe the "discussion" that followed, but the funny part was that about a week later, we heard the exact same joke on the TV show, *Roseanne.*

After a laugh, my wife said, "Honestly, Matthew, you should be writing for these shows."

That was not the first time I had heard that from my family and friends, but somehow, that time, it stuck. From then on, I have studied the nature of jokes and humor.

A few years later, I even wondered if I could write for late night television shows. That is, take a headline and turn it into a quick, smart, snappy one or two liner. Then do it several times a day for 5 days a week. As an experiment, I tried to write just one-a-day for a month. It was exhausting. I could blame full-time teaching and family responsibilities, but the fact was, it's dammed hard work.

Still, I had a minor success.

My experiment with writing topical jokes came during the presidential impeachment process of the 1990s. That was the trial for President Bill Clinton, who had famously said he tried marijuana once, but "didn't inhale." Liar.

He also lied about having an affair with a White House intern named Monica Lewinsky. They had sex a few times in the Oval Office, and he was impeached for lying about it. Can you imagine? Now *that's* a high crime!

My Joke?

"You know. President Clinton and Monica Lewinsky make the perfect couple. He doesn't inhale, and she doesn't swallow."

Two nights later, David Letterman told a similar joke on his *Late Night* Show. I was rather proud of myself and came to the conclusion that I could make a living writing jokes! But there was the pre-school tuition to pay, the student loans to pay, and my wonderful job as a teacher.

Of course I didn't just stop writing jokes and riffing in my classrooms, as this book demonstrates. And lest a good liberal is offended by my vulgar Clinton joke, well, at least he had a cat.

I like it when my presidents have pets. The closest Donald Trump has gotten is the two Golden Relievers he had in a Moscow hotel room.

Long Form Jokes

As I dabbled in the art of joke writing, this bold new thing appeared on the interwebs: Facebook. My inner stand-up comic had a stage! Anything funny I said in the classroom could be re-written and posted for a larger audience. Even better, I could write longer bits. Here are a few.

Cats

Why do we give cats cans of beef, turkey, or tuna to eat? I mean have you ever seen a cat take down cow or snag a tuna out of the sea? No, of course not. We should feed cats things more along their natural order. Things like canned bluebird. Minced mice. Chopped chipmunk. Maybe a nice squirrel, mole, and songbird medley.

Can you see the signs in the store? "This week's special! Gourmet Goldfish Entree with Grilled Guppy Gills."

This is why cats attack our toes when we sleep; they really have no choice but to punish us.

The biggest thing we should feed a cat is a duck. I saw a cat take on a duck once. Old Tom ruffled a few feathers, but the duck royally goosed him.

Clutter

House full of clutter? Garage overflowing? Maybe you need a black hole! They're cheaper than you think. We here at Light Benders Unlimited will deliver and set up the perfect-sized Gravitational Suck Machine for your needs. Then, once all your problems have been spaghettified and lost to another universe, we will remove it all with our Little Bang Bots.

So if you no longer find joy in your crap, call LBU for a free estimate (Not responsible for lost children or pets). Ask your physicist if a black hole is right for you.

English & Facebook

English teachers on Facebook be like: Comment how we first met in a 3000-4000 word essay. Be sure to underline the topic sentence of each paragraph and underline your thesis twice. Use appropriate MLA format for your page one heading, but APA style for any and all citations. Please attach an annotated bibliography instead of a "Works Cited" page. Under no circumstance should you use the Chicago Style Manual – unless you plan to publish the comment in a peer-reviewed journal that requires that particular style (please message me if such is the case, as I will expect to be included as a co-author). Comments must employ the Oxford comma, when appropriate, or face immediate deletion. Two such infractions may be cause for "unfriending". As you work through your seventh draft, be sure to channel the spirits of *Strunk and White*. And finally, yes – spelling counts. Thank You.

New Course Idea!

Logic 490: Paradox Writing and Construction. A systematic study of paradoxes through history, from the Garden of Eden Incident to Nero's Fiddle to Nixon's Resignation. Said study will establish rules and models for students to use in the development of their own paradoxical answers to questions about the meaning of life and/or those posed by Sunday Morning News Show hosts. Central to the course will be Picasso's statement: "Art is the lie that enables us to understand the truth." 3 Credit Hours.

Religion

I'm thinking of starting a cult. Is there anything special I need to do? Any papers to file with some authorities or government? Is there an organizational waiting time, or am I free to begin gathering followers this very day?

Also, as all great religions began as cults, how long must I wait before rebranding my cult as a religion? Does anyone have to die to initiate the process? Does it have to be me? If not, look for information on THE CHURCH OF THE WOLFE in the near future. That's all.

The Bright, Bright Future

Many of my generation are bummed out because we thought we'd have flying cars by now. We got the idea from a silly, 1960s cartoon called *The Jetsons*. Yeah, that's all I need. I get cut off all the time from the left and right. Can you imagine getting cutoff from above? From *below*!? I mean the middle finger would no longer do it. Someone drop his Levitating Lexus in my windshield, *Hell*! I'm giving him the pinkie of death!

But I never wanted a flying car. I wanted a gun that could vaporize people. I saw it in a sci-fi show on our black and white TV. I was like 6. An alien drew his heat, pulled the trigger, and ZAP!, the human was nothing but a few smoldering cinders on a Persian rug. I was scared to death. Just stared at the TV a while. Had nightmares. The next day, I realized the only way to dump the scaredy-cat in me was to plan on buying a human-vaporizer as soon as they started making them.

I'm still waiting.

My only hope now is that vaporizer guns get here before flying cars. Cut me off from below with your Buick Balloon and I'm gonna vaporize your ass.

Anecdotes

Of course, with a life like mine I have plenty of humorous and true stories to tell. Here are a few of my favorites.

Way Out West

I am sitting alone at a bar in Missoula, Montana, sipping a local whiskey and clearing 300 miles of back-road travel from my head. The Parkinson's tremors in my right hand flare up a bit, so I fidget with the tumbler of "Sudden Wisdom" with the left. It is past time for my next dose of dope, the dopamine that replaces the holy chemicals my brain is stingy with these days.

I jam my shaky paw into my jeans pocket for the stainless steel pill safe that dangles from my key ring with the key to Jeep Shiloh. I keep it simple when I travel.

I screw off the lid and shake a pill out onto a cocktail napkin I have already snatched from the backside of the bar. Then I screw the lid back on and shove the ring, safe, and key back in my pocket.

After 8 weeks of travel, after dozens of late evenings in bars from Florida to Alaska, I have a ritual. Washing down the dope with whiskey before supper and bed is a pleasant way to say "Fuck You" to this miserable disease.

Just as I pop the pill and raise the glass, a beautiful woman sits down on the stool beside me. As the alcohol tumbles over my lip and teeth, as it flows over the tip of my tongue to the bitter tablet, the woman says, "Kind of early for the Viagra isn't it?"

I nearly spit the fizzing brew of dope and "Wisdom" across the oak bar. Bravely, I suck it all back and swallow hard. Then I turn to gaze on the siren who sang for my attention. Hazel eyes, bleached blonde hair, dark red lipstick, about my age but a looker to be sure. The road has been lonely, and temptation stretches out on the bar like a cat after the kill.

I hold up my right hand, the tremors wriggling through a few fingers as if playing an invisible trumpet.

"That little pill helps me with my Parkinson's disease," I reply, "Not my love life."

Her expression, with a tilt of the head and strong smile, shows inquisitiveness, not sympathy. This is a relief.

"But you know," I continue, still holding up my tanned, shaky mitt, "One night with me and you'll never go back to your vibrator."

Fashion

When my Aunt Sue broke her leg, I dropped everything to follow the ambulance to the hospital. I had been doing yard work in my favorite, worn tennis shoes, but there was no time to change. When we reached the ER, we spent about 6 hours on X-rays and CT scans; then she was moved to a room to await surgery the next day. Once Sue was settled, I decided to head home. As I left, she asked me to take her purse with me. Sue's "purse" was a huge, gold, vinyl bag with a kaleidoscope of colorful, plastic gemstones. Without a thought, I slung it over my shoulder and headed for the elevator. On my way down to the lobby, the elevator stopped at the 3rd floor, and a very attractive woman in a sharp business jacket and skirt stepped on. As we continued toward the ground level, I caught her eyeing me from the side. Thinking I might score a date, I glanced at my lift companion, smiled, and said, "Hi." She looked me over once again, and said, "You know, those shoes don't go with that bag."

Neighbor Management

Then there was the day I looked out my back window and spotted two baby skunks playing in a fern patch next to a stack of firewood. Those tiny pole-kittens were as cute as any feline kitties, as they wrestled and rolled in the soft fronds and dirt. I must have watched these two critters for a half an hour.

Of course there was a downside. Somewhere in my yard was a mama skunk, an adult who could stink up the sweet scents of spring.

The next couple of days, as I went about my business of yard work, I always gave the woodpile and ferns a wide berth. In other words we got along just fine.

One day, while I was assembling a new lawnmower in my front yard, a Lexus pulled up and the electric, tinted, driver's-side window slid down with a hum. I saw the face of one of my neighbors, a lawyer who lived in a more affluent neighborhood just beyond mine. Without a greeting or a howdy do, he blurted out, "You know you got skunks living in your yard?!"

As I walked closer to his car, I replied, "Well, yes. I do. Cute rascals."

"Cute? What if they come down the road and spray a kid?"

"I guess the kid would know to leave skunks alone," I chuckled.

The Lexus lawyer didn't laugh. He instead said, "You know of anyway to get rid of them?"

"No. I don't. But I have a cousin who'd know. I'll call him."

"See that you do."

The window whirred back up and the Lexus esquire took off for a day of defending the guilty and suing the innocent.

Aggravated though I was, I did, in fact call my cousin that very night.

"Dana," I asked after we exchanged pleasantries, "I've got a mother skunk and two of her babies living on my place."

"And I reckon they is living in your firewood. They love to make dens under a wood pile," Dana answered in his southern West Virginia cadence.

Dana was the last living mountain man I knew of. I wasn't a bit surprised he knew the score.

"Yes," I said. "And we're getting along just fine, but some of my neighbors are upset, which I think is a good reason to leave them well enough alone."

"Well, yes," he said. "Skunks will keep the neighbors away."

"But if I decided to get rid of them, what do you think would be the best way?"

"Well, I tell ya, Matt. Go down to the farm supply store and get you two live traps."

"Okay..."

"Take the traps out to Beech Fork State Park, and catch you a couple of coyotes. You set them coyotes free in your yard, and they'll take care of the skunks!"

I agreed that his was indeed a fine plan and said I'd give it careful consideration. A pair of hungry coyotes would certainly solve the problem, though it might raise a nasal nightmare for a couple of days.

The next day I took a long break reading my mail in the front yard. Soon enough the Lexus pulled up and the window wound down.

"Did you talk to your cousin?"

"I did."

"And?"

"He said we should get a couple of traps, catch some coyotes, set them loose here, and turn the skunks into coyote chow."

The lawyer looked surprised, but I could see his mind mull it over for about two seconds. Then he said, "But what about the cats and small dogs in the neighborhood?"

"Well that *is* another problem. When you solve a problem in nature it often leads to more problems. But it's better than skunks I guess."

"Ridiculous," he replied. Then the window hummed up and the car pulled away. I chuckled, because I assumed that was the end of it.

Besides, I hadn't seen the skunks in a couple of days. Skunks generally don't stay in one place for long. The kittens had grown enough, and the little family had moved on.

I was surprised a few days later when the Lexus pulled up in front of my house once again. Poor guy was still worrying over the skunks.

"So if you do what your cousin suggested," he said, " how would you get rid of the coyotes?"

I leaned in close to the window opening, grinned real big, and said, "wolves."

My Five Favorite Jokes

Over my lifetime, I have accumulated hundreds of jokes in my head, jokes I didn't write. The fun with standards like these, is telling them in your own words, with your own spin, as I have done many times. Over the years, these five have become my favorites.

Number Five!

At a wedding a few weeks ago, I sat next to my great aunt. Just as the newly-weds kissed, she elbowed me and said, "You're next." Then yesterday I wound up sitting nest to her at a funeral, so, just as they closed the casket, I nudged her and said, "You're next!"

I've been cut from her will.

Number Four!

The other day I went horseback riding, but it didn't go well. In fact, I thought I would die. From the start the horse was unsteady and bucked a bit. He was also unmanageable. I couldn't get him to turn or slow no matter what I did with the reins. He just kept going straight at a fast gallop. I looked up ahead and saw a busy highway, and I thought my heart would stop. Again, I tried to rein him in, even standing in the stirrups. That didn't work either, and suddenly I fell off his back to the hard ground. Worse, my left foot was caught in the stirrup. Still, that horse kept going right for the highway, dragging me along on my back and bouncing off the ground. I started yelling, "Whoa" and "Help." I even saw my miserable life flash before my eyes. Dear, God, in heaven," I yelled out, "save me from the hands of death." I closed my eyes and braced for the worst.

And then, miracle of miracles, that old horse came to an abrupt stop! Everything was quiet. I slowly opened my eyes. Standing over me was the Wal-Mart manager with the power cord in his hand. Thank God he had unplugged the beast in the nick of time.

Number Three!

A man goes on vacation and asks his neighbor to check on his cat each day. A few days later, the man calls his neighbor to see how things are going.

"How's my cat?" he asks.

"Your cat died," the neighbor blurts out.

"What? I can't believe it!" The man cries for several minutes.

When he finally regains his composure, he chews out his neighbor for being rude: "What's wrong with you? You should have prepared me by saying something like 'The cat's on the roof, and we can't get her down.' That way I would have called tomorrow to see what's happening. Then you could have told me she was still on the roof and wouldn't eat. And, when

I called on the third day, I would have been prepared for the worst when you told me she had died."

"You're right," the neighbor says. "I'm really sorry. You've taught me a valuable lesson."

Well, good," the man replies. "Now, how's my mother?"

"She's on the roof, and we can't get her down."

Number Two!

My uncle Joe learned a valuable lesson last week. He had a job interview for his dream position, and he took a short cut out an old country road. Halfway to the next town, the right rear tire blew out. Joe quickly pulled over to the right, but not very far, for there was a wide drainage ditch on that side. On the other side of the ditch was a high chain-link fence, and well beyond that, up on a small hill, was an old stone building. As Joe well knew, this was the state mental hospital.

Joe got out of his car, took off his suit jacket, and folded it neatly on the car seat. He then rolled up his shirtsleeves, opened the trunk, and pulled out the jack and the tire iron. As he turned to move to the flat, Joe was surprised to see a woman standing on the other side of the fence, the fingers of both hands tightly gripping the links. She wore a stern and stoic expression, and she was dressed in gray sweats – the standard uniform of the mental patients.

Joe said to her, "Oh. Hello. How are you this morning?" She did not answer but stared at him. This unnerved him a bit, but Joe went on with the job of changing the tire.

Soon he had the car jacked up and the flat tire off. The lug nuts were nestled safely in the wheel cover. The woman watched his every move but never made a sound.

Then, just after Joe got the spare in place, disaster struck, for as he reached for a lug nut, he bumped the wheel cover and watched helplessly as the cover and nuts slipped to the edge of the ditch and then toppled over. He could see the glint of each of the five nuts in the sunshine just before they plopped into several inches of mud and green scummy ditch water.

Joe couldn't believe his eyes.

Joe peered into the ditch, gently kneeled with the knees of his suit pants in the dirt, and tried to reach into the muck in the ditch. He couldn't quite make it, so he leaned forward and stretched even farther. The tips of his fingers just began to explore the mud when he lost his balance and tipped over into the ditch headfirst.

SLOP! PLOP! SPLAT! went Joe.

By the time he rolled over and crawled out of the ditch, Joe was covered in thick mud and green scum. He scraped mud from his eyes and surveyed the mess. Some orange goop of an unknown origin was smeared across his chest. Filthy water ran out of his hair.

Realizing his dream job was now history, Joe screamed. Then he kicked his car, the flat tire, and the jack. The jack toppled over and the right rear end of the car crashed to the ground narrowly missing his foot. He kicked the car again. Then he began to cry. To blubber. To wail.

Joe sank to the ground in his grief and sobbed uncontrollably for several minutes.

Finally, as he began to compose himself, Joe leaned back against his car and began to take stock of his situation. That's when he realized the woman in the gray sweats was still watching him.

"Why are you staring at me like that?" he shouted.

She replied, "Why didn't you just take a nut from each of the other wheels to hold the spare on until you got to town?"

Joe was astonished. He thought about it for a moment, and realized she was right. He had ruined his suit and job prospects for nothing.

Joe looked up at her again and said, "That's brilliant! Why in the world are you in there?"

She replied, "I may be crazy, but I'm not stupid."

My Number One Favorite Joke!

An old man sits alone on a park bench. He has long, flowing white hair and a long white beard. His clothes are tattered.

A young man walks over and sits down next to him. After a few minutes of watching the birds and joggers in the park, he looks over to the old man and says, "Old Man, they say you are very smart and very wise. Why is that?"

The Old Man turns to the younger fellow, and, with a twinkle in his eyes, replies, "I've read many books and attended many universities."

"Then why, Old Man," the youth asks, "do you live alone, in a cave, in the middle of the forest, eating nothing but nuts and roots?"

Without hesitation the Old Man replies, "I've read many books and attended many universities."

Melodic Punch Lines

As a musician, I have always kept my ear open for jokes with a melody for a punchline. These are obviously rare, because they must be melodies the typical listener will recognize when you sing the line. Then, when you try to write them down for a book, wowzers! Still, here are two that I think survive such ill-treatment.

The Suicide

A not-at-all famous trumpet player was touring Europe with a mediocre band no one had ever heard of. He was an alcoholic who was always late and who told strings of offensive jokes. When the band reached Paris, they decided they had had quite enough of him. So, they found a suitable replacement and left the scoundrel behind. Upon discovering he'd been abandoned at the hotel, the trumpet player did the expected. He went on a three-day drinking binge.

On the third evening he woke up with a massive hangover and realized he was broke, homeless, alone, and without hope. Certain that he had nothing to live for, the trumpeter decided to end his life. He crawled out of bed and staggered to the doors that led to his room's balcony, some five floors above the street.

But when the trumpet player stepped out into the evening, he was stunned by the view before him. There glowed the famous lights of Paris and the wondrous Eiffel Tower. And in the distance the sunset painted the sky with yellows, reds, and oranges. Simply, it was the most beautiful sight the trumpeter had ever witnessed.

In that transcendental moment he realized he did not have to take his life. He knew he could turn his fortunes around. He knew he could be a better man and a fine musician. He could make a difference in the world, dammit.

Thus inspired, the man rushed back into his room to retrieve his trumpet, for he wished to serenade the City of Lights with his music.

Back on the balcony, the trumpeter blew air through the horn and fingered the valves a few times to warm up a bit. Then, gazing at the Eiffel Tower, he drew his lips into the proper position, took a deep breath, and began playing.

He played the melody to "Somewhere Over the Rainbow" from the movie *The Wizard of Oz*: Daa daa—- dadadada--daa. Daa dadada daa. — And so on up to the melodic bridge of the song whereupon he stopped cold, for he could not remember what came next.

This angered him a bit. After all, how could he forget the bridge? He had played it thousands of times before. Muscle memory should have taken over. He decided to try again, Daa Daa dadadadada- playing the first 8 measures of the song, but once again stopping at the bridge with no clue as to what came next.

Furious, he yelled a few cuss words in English and French.

A crowd gathered five floors below waiting to see what would happen next.

The trumpet player tried yet again. This time rushing through the song to get to the bridge as quickly as possible. Dadadadadadadadadada Daa. And nothing happened. He simply could not recall what came next.

Outraged, the trumpeter threw his trumpet to the concrete floor of the balcony, jumped over the railing, and plunged to the street below.

Lying on the pavement, crumpled and dying, the last thing he heard was the distinctive sound of the siren of a French ambulance:

Naa – naa – naa – naa – naa – naa

The Maestro

Beethoven sat at the piano in his studio, pecking at the keys, when his wife waltzed in and began dusting.

"Woman," he barked, "must you clean now?!"

"I'm trying to finish the cleaning before the weekend, you half-deaf fool," she bullied back.

"Well scram, can't you see I'm working here?"

"Work? You? Ha! You should quit composing and take on more students. Bring in some money so we can hire a maid and a cook!"

"You lazy wife. I'm starting a new symphony, my fifth, and as soon I find the perfect melody, I will compose the greatest symphony ever!"

"Greatest ever! You are indeed a fool."

"You just watch. With this symphony I will be famous for centuries to come!"

To which Beethoven's wife laughed: "Ha. Ha. Ha. HAAAAA!"

Practical Jokes

Liberal Laugh

I don't play many practical jokes. The payback paranoia weighs too heavily, as I wait for the victim to return fire at some unspecified moment in the future. I am not a ninja who can remain constantly alert and hear the blow coming from behind me while I make my tea – or Jack and Coke.

For me, a good practical joke is one played on a good-natured victim who will take it in stride. Better yet is the joke that can be performed anonymously and   with a vague notion of a victim. A practical joke also needs a large audience. Why go to the trouble of a stunt if it won't have more than a few friends to acknowledge your cleverness and grit? Yes. There is much to consider when you search for the perfect plot to shame and embarrass others for a cheap laugh.

Based on those criteria, then, my best practical joke was one I pulled during my junior year at Marshall University. That was the year that the main administrative building was under renovation, and makeshift offices were set up in other buildings. My own college, The College of Liberal Arts, housed its dean and staff in the lobby of Smith Hall, a large classroom building that I walked through several times a day.

Over the summer, construction workers had erected a couple of walls and installed a flimsy door to create a temporary office space (that space is now an art gallery). By the time classes began in August, most everyone knew where COLA was now located, except for students and visitors. For this reason, a sign of sorts was placed over the door.

Now, this "sign" was as flimsy and temporary as anything else. It looked to me as though a student assistant had grabbed some light brown construction paper and a pair of scissors and fashioned her own letters. They were about four inches tall and a bit bubbly, as was the fashion of the time. She had then stapled these letters over the door in such an order as to spell out:

THE COLLEGE OF
LIBERAL ARTS

When I first saw it, I was impressed by the simplicity and practicality of it all. Then I was struck with grand inspiration.

It just so happened that the dividers in one of my notebooks were similar in texture and color to the paper letters over the door. So, after office hours, and after securing scissors and a stapler, I cut out a letter of my own and added it to one of the words above the door. And that is how I became a student in

THE COLLEGE OF
LIBERAL FARTS

It was indeed a glorious moment when I stepped back to see the fruits of my labor. Then, when two fellow students walked by and turned to see what I was looking at, they burst out laughing. Well. That was a moment of rapture I shall never forget.

The best part?

Though my handiwork was done in late August, it remained for the world to see until mid-April, a nearly 8 month run. Apparently all the more "responsible" people on campus already knew where the office was and never looked at the sign. Still others probably read what they expected to see and missed the slightly off-color "F" in the mix or the crowded letter spacing. But who knows how many students and visitors got a chuckle over my installation? Hundreds? A thousand? More?

As for me, that fall and winter turned out to be exceedingly rough for a number of reasons. Walking past my little display of disobedience each day gave me a smile and a reason to keep pushing.

April 1ˢᵗ Facebook Post

Hey all. I'd appreciate your good thoughts today. I'll be having toe transplant surgery this afternoon. Simply put, the doctors hope to solve my Parkinson's balance problems by swapping my big toes. I'm the first to undergo this experimental procedure, and they have informed me that I may have to trade my flip-flops for flop-flips. Even at that, it seems worth the trouble to keep me from falling every few weeks (ceilings are rather boring to look at, as you may imagine). Should this procedure work, watch for a "Go fund me" so that I can swap the clutch and the gas pedal on Jeep Shiloh. Anyway, thanks and peace to all of you.

Note: I got several well wishes and "Thoughts and Prayers" in the comments. One fellow commented: "I've never heard of such a thing, and doubt it would work, but I guess it's worth a try. Good Luck."

Random Pieces

Your Morning Fruit-Loops:
A Response to the Pop Culture
Misuse of the Word "Surreal"

If you dream you and a lion are walking together in a beautiful meadow on a sunny day, that is a dream.

If you dream the lion chases, catches, and eats you, that is a nightmare.

If you dream you, a lion, and a zebra are playing poker in a swimming pool with onion slices for chips, that is surrealism (The zebra is cheating by the way).

If you dream the lion starts to eat you, but all his teeth fall out, so he asks you about the meaning of life while you both wait for the train to work, that's absurdism.

If you wake in the morning, having had any of these dreams, only to find you are now a lionfish trapped in a tiny fishbowl and perched on the edge of a seat on a fast-moving train to work, that's Kafkaesque.

If you have no dreams, feel that you have no control over your life, and see a woman with a tattoo of a white rabbit on her shoulde and wish to follow her rather than go to work, then wake up, Neo. You're in The Matrix.

Me And Golf Through The Ages

10-year-old me: Who watches golf on TV? This is boring. Going outside to play.

18-year-old me: OK. So an hour on a color TV is kind of cool, kind of relaxing. Time to practice my drum solo.

27-year-old me: Golf is old boy networking, corporate bullshit. Hmmm. Still. There is this sort of Zen thing here.

35-year-old me: Tiger who?

40-year-old me: Dear sports commentators, Woods is NOT a Zen master. Close, but he's too emotional when he screws up. Phil Jackson is the Zen Master in sports now. Read a book or two, will ya. Meanwhile, I'll watch TV to see if he *does* become a zen master.

45-year-old-me: Tiger blew it playing holes *off* the course. And golf courses are destroying the earth with all the chemicals, fertilizers, waste of water.... Still, The Masters is beautiful to look at with a cable TV signal.

Me today: The Masters. New HDTV with sound bar. Nance's voice a sweet baritone. Birdies singing from trees. Tiger may make a comeback. 15 minutes in: Zzzzzzz.

Don't get angry. Write a post.

There is a famous urban myth about a businessman in the 1930s who wanted to insult a competitor for spreading vicious lies about him. Remember, this was a time when secretaries took dictation then typed up the letters for their bosses to sign. In this case the letter read:

Dear Mr. Smith,

Being a gentleman, I cannot use the words that best describe you. Being a lady, my secretary cannot be expected to type them. You however, being neither, know exactly what I mean.

–Yours, JT

That's fine, I suppose, but it doesn't exactly cut it in the 21st century, and I don't have a secretary.

But I do have Facebook.

One April day, I got bullied over my Parkinson's disease by a woman in the grocery store. I wasn't really angry or hurt, but I used it to create awareness about a chronic illness that plagues millions of US citizens. This stunt elicited sympathy (which was never my intention) and lead to discussions and at least 25 shares.

"Dear odious, impatient, ignorant, grocery store diva, I could sense your frustration behind me in the cookie aisle. I was worried your shopping buggy would soon bounce from the backs of my ankles. And

I could hear your too-many-cigarettes-shredded-throat whisper as you said to your shopping companion, "If he doesn't move it, I'm gonna kill him and run him over!" Nice. You see, you old nag, that was as fast as I could safely walk today. I have Parkinson's symptoms, and, while tremors get all the attention, we Parkies have other symptoms, too. Loss of balance is one of them. If I had rushed at your command (I know you wanted me to hear your raspy "whisper"), I might well have fallen and pulled down a pile of Fig Newtons with me. Then you'd have been stuck! (BTW: given your tremendous girth, you really shouldn't have been in the cookie aisle to begin with.) Now, normally I wouldn't take the time to write this –or the effort (my right hand is so rigid today, another common symptom, that I'm typing this with my left hand) – but today, April 1st, is the first day of Parkinson's Awareness Month. Maybe my friends will share this, and their friends and so on until it winds up in your news feed. In the meantime, taste my doubt as to you having any just cause for existing on this planet."

Poetry

Tennyson Takes a Bullet

Once upon a midnight dreary, in a basement dank and eerie,
I stumbled over a volume of poetic lore.
With eyes so red and weary, I examined a book quite dreary,
For there was a hole in its spine no worm could ever bore,
A hole so deep and ratty, every page was creased and tore – n.
Only this and nothing more.

Thumbing through its many pages, looking for some hermits and some sages,
I found Alfred, Lord Tennyson, a poet whom I never did adore.
His photo showed a figure bald, also unsmiling and unribald.
Such a sorry visage recalled a poet me thought to be a snore
(Though commentary by Charles French was equal on that score,
More or less forgotten, forevermore).

Guinevere and the Grail, Lancelot and some ale
Were the subjects of this dusty book of yore.
Upon the title page I started peering, long I stood there fearing
<u>Idylls of the King</u>, Macmillan and Company, 1934.
Truly, thought I, this is a book I should ignore.
Tis only dullness here and nothing more.

Still, the rips in the gutter which made Arthur stutter
Thrilled me – filled me with fantastic terrors I never felt before.
What bit of violence could attempt to silence
Alfred, Lord Tennyson, like nothing heretofore?
Perhaps it was a raven's beak and nothing more.
Perhaps a raven's beak, nothing more.

Presently my soul grew stronger; hesitating then no longer,
I crept upstairs and down the hall to my father's chamber door.
There I caught him napping, so gently I started rapping,
But gave up, went in, and tap, tap, tapped him with that book of lore.
"This book has tasted disaster, tis a mystery I must explore."

Quoth my father, "Nevermore."

"But surely," I snipped, "you know the saddle stitch is ripped
And there's a small hole in its backside leading to its core."
"Don't call me 'Shirely'," came the reply a tad bit surly.
"T'was an accident before you were born and nothing more.
T'was an incident without rhyme, just a bore.
Oh, and on your way out, *close the door*."

"Prophet," said I. "You *do* know! Could you not your eldest son show?"
(A smile spread across his face as the memory reached its shore).
"This volume reveals Arthur's passing and the treasure he was massing,
But this hole, this hole! Forgive me but I must implore!
There's family history here, and I really must know more!
Quoth my father, "Ah, what the hell."

He said, "Distinctly do I remember, t'was some dark and bleak December
When my evil stepmother came rapping at my bedroom door.
She held aloft her trusty revolver, her handy little problem solver,
For she filled her time shooting rats at river's shore.
Tin cans too, but mostly rats at river's shore.
Only this and nothing more.

"'Son,' she inquired sweetly, 'would you help me,' she added meekly,
'would you clean my little gun, the cylinder, and the bore?'
'Golly,' I replied. 'I'd love to,' I lied.
Peace in the household was worth the chore.
She handed me her worn revolver then waltzed back out my door.
Darkness there and nothing more.

"I pulled out a rod and some patches to wad,
And the skinny brush with the stiff bristles of a boar.
Then I picked up said gun, and BANG!, my head, it spun,
For the weapon went off with an echoing roar!
For the weapon went off and a bullet did soar!
I perched. I sat. I did nothing more.

"I was certainly stunned and significantly out gunned,
And smoke slowly settled upon the clothing that I wore.
My ears were brightly ringing from the bullet's wayward zinging,
And I searched myself for blood and some gore.
Then I searched the room and of my stepmother I swore,
'Frosty old hoar!'

"I searched the shelves upon the wall, looked for a hole and leaden ball,
And found that book knocked from his seat and laying upon the floor.
The spine was still smoking, Lord Tennyson near choking,
And again I cursed that matronly conspirator,
For the bullet got through more of Tennyson than I ever had before.
Only this and nothing more.
Now: on your way out – close that door."

Haiku

I tried to write hai
Ku today, but the syllab
Les refused muchly.

You're a butterfly.
Labeled and pinned to cardboard,
You're *MY* butterfly.

Shuffle through darkness
To wear off insomnia.
Toes find the chair leg.

I once loved the sound
Of rain tapping on my house,
But now my roof leaks.

Last night the monster
Under my bed belched and said
"Dust bunnies! Yummy!"

Withdrawing my tongue
From the mermaid's salty mouth,
I hum a few scales.

Three Word Haiku

Ventriloquism:
Onomatopoetic
Pandemonium.

Adaptive Haiku

(5) Thus Darwin did speak:
(8) "Tis not the fittest who survive,
(6) But those who can adapt."

[Unfinished Haiku]
Jungle sound from deep in throat,
Kitten stalks the bird.

–Clark Wolfe

Pie-ku

Friday night pizza,
Eat a tummy yummy with
Pepperoni eyes.

Mycoo (MY-coo) A poetic form invented by Matthew C. Wolfe, Ph.D., in which syllables are arranged in lines of 5-4-3-2-1 and which ends with a subtle complaint ("coo" def. as a "soft murmur"). Quite useful when a haiku won't do, or when 17 syllables is two too many. Stick *that* in the OED!

Thanksgiving Mycoo

So stuff those bellies.
Eat those turkeys.
Launch a war
Against
Yams.

Nature Mycoo
(Words by Beverly Delidow,
arranged by Matthew Wolfe)

A grand woodpecker
Uses the rain
Gutter for
His love
Drum.

"Normal" Mycoo

Furnace on the fritz.
Temperatures
Dropping fast.
Too damn
Cold!

Pretty little wren
Sits on my red
Jeep. Takes a
Big, white
Dump.

Blue butterflies dance
For their maker.
We are just
In the
Way.

And now for few more words from ~~our sponsor~~ My Father, The Land Surveyor:

Legal Description

Beginning as a point in time and space, in an obscure corner of the universe, and being an infinite distance from the supreme bench-mark around which all galaxies revolve, which is not recorded in any map book ever heard of. Continuing from said point in an obscure direction – north, east, south, and west being disputed terms, bounded by neighboring travelers in the Milky Way, a distance not to exceed ones imagination, to the point of beginning. And containing who knows how many acres, this being a geodetic survey and who understands that?

Said parcel having been conveyed by the Creator to mankind by contract, date of which is unknown, and recorded only in the big record room in the sky, book and page numbers being of no consequence.

Default now having been made on such contract due to improper maintenance of premises, and squatters-rights being asserted, eviction proceedings are hereby begun under the terms of the Treaty of Armageddon.

– Clark Wolfe

PART III
The Storyteller

The Seven Headless Dwarfs

The outdoors, "backstage" area of Disney World stood as a boundary between the organized chaos of family entertainment and the natural order of a wetlands. Alligators to the north. Peter Pan to the south. I was a teenager in limbo. My own family for this trek to the Magic Kingdom was the roughly 100 members and supporters of The Barboursville High School Invincible Marching Band. I was a snare drummer running on little sleep. Actually, we were all a bit groggy. An over-night, 800-mile bus trip meant an all-night party of card games, pranks, silly songs, and serious make-out sessions on tour buses.

Now we were a bleary-eyed mob caught in the brilliant Florida sun, ready for Space Mountain and the Pirates of the Caribbean. There was just one little obligation we had to meet first: march in a parade through the lame "Main Street, USA" section of the park.

After warm-ups and inspection, we waited in our hot uniforms and listened to people laughing and enjoying life on the other side of a tall wooden fence. It was the eternal musicians' madness of "Hurry up and wait", and we were missing out on precious minutes in the "Happiest Place on Earth".

Suddenly a nearby gate in the fence burst open and the Seven Dwarfs marched in. They were in single file, Doc leading the way, of course, and Dopey at the rear. It was a glorious moment for me and my band mates, and we hailed them with "ohs" and "ahs." Then things went south in a hurry.

When the gate slammed shut behind Dopey, the Dwarfs broke stride and soon resembled a small herd of staggering, drunken elves. These chaotic and colorful creatures were all headed for the one bit of shade to be found, an arthritic maple tree with a picnic table beneath. There a large water cooler and a stack of paper cups waited on the table.

Just as they closed in on this diminished oasis, Grumpy decapitated himself.

Which is to say the man in the costume removed his head. Well not *his* head. The head of Grumpy.

I had always assumed Grumpy had a violent bent, but I figured he'd do in Doc first. Self-beheading is a rather desperate call for help.

And there was nothing bashful about Bashful when he popped his top.

One might hope that Sneezy would at least sneeze his head off, but no, he removed it with his hands just like the others. Damned conformist.

Slowly (much slower than I care to admit) I realized these were real men in costumes, men who looked nothing like the lovable Dwarfs. One was, I am sure, an escaped convict from a Georgia chain gang. He and two others were white. The other four appeared to be Hispanic. All seven wore sweat like cheap make-up. Even now they could not wipe away the sweat, for their fingers were lost in fake-hand gloves.

As the shock began to ease, I looked at the thin and sweaty men inside. They were of average height and wore T-shirts and wife beaters as well as bandanas around their (real) heads to keep the sweat out of their eyes – a scruffy lot to be sure. The Dwarf trousers came up to their armpits and were held in place by wide suspenders, contrasting their youthful faces with outlines resembling old men with their pants hiked up to their chins.

Sleepy carried his head up-side-down by a bottom edge, near the neck. The white beard fell across Sleepy's half-moon eyes like a bad comb-over on an elderly stoner.

Dopey meanwhile carried his head in front of him, clutching it by the huge ears. Far from stupid, Dopey's inner dude looked like William Shakespeare, complete with a goatee and a little earring.

Sleepy's inner man sported a three-day growth of dark whiskers, not the virgin white beard of his outer-narcoleptic.

Once they reached the picnic table, the man-dwarfs placed their heads on the grass in a nice, straight row. It looked like a headhunter's wet dream. Then they removed their gloves and tossed them beside the freakish heads. The hand-gloves held their shape. This created the bloodless crime scene of a mass murderer with OCD tendencies. All the hard-boiled detective needed to do now was look for the "nice guy next door" with seven headless and handless bodies stuffed into his freezers.

Then, horror of horrors: Happy produced a pack of cigarettes and a lighter from somewhere inside his oversized Dwarf pants – I try not to imagine – and soon five of the lot were puffing away, including

Dopey, whom I am sure caved in to peer pressure. Shame on you, Happy!

Obviously it was break time for the crew, their state mandated 10 minutes per four hours of work. The little-tall-men worked for hourly wages, a weekly paycheck. "I owe. I owe. It's off to work I go!" So much for our carefree diamond miners.

And there we were, a group of high schoolers quietly watching – amused, bewildered, and disillusioned. It was like discovering Santa was really just your parents, only somehow a little worse. A part of the Magic Kingdom lost its magic just as we stood at its threshold. Adulthood nipped at our imaginations, and the scent of melancholy, sweat, and smoke permeated the humid air.

Suddenly we were called to attention. There were four short blasts of the Drum Major's whistle and my brothers in drums and I began playing a cadence. Then BOOM! The gates opened, and we marched out onto the stage of Disney World, leaving the seven half-dwarfs behind.

As we made our way down Main Street playing some tune from a Disney movie, I wondered something. Where was Snow White? What was her deal? Was she too good for the backstage likes of Dwarfs and drummers? I summoned a vision of Snow White and Cinderella sitting half-dressed in an air-conditioned dressing room and trash-talking Minnie Mouse while they smoked a joint. It turns out adult fantasies can be damn good, too.

Hi ho!

And now a few words ABOUT my father from his future mother-in-law, my grandmother, when he barked at her chocolate cake during his very first visit to her home. (And people wonder what my mother saw in him.)

I think you're more monkey than Wolfe.

– Verna Akers

Hot Turkeys

My mother was a teacher. Dad should have been; he taught me a lot of amazing things (like how to survey with a Boy Scout compass). As a result, family vacations always had an educational component. The parental figures dragged me to battleships, plantations, monuments, museums, and Plymouth Rock.

Plymouth Rock, it should be noted, was kept in a cage to protect it from vandals. The cage allowed the tide to come in to kiss the rock and made an odd sort of stone zoo with one large specimen. The rock had even been branded, "1620" having been carved into its smooth surface. This created a simulation of a legend laced with mythology: a bit of nature too sacred to be sacred. I walked away with an uneasy sadness for that Puritan relic. Dad meanwhile chirped something about how did they know it was the actual rock the pilgrims stepped on as they exited their landing craft. He argued that the pilgrims weren't the brightest buckles on the hat. "Who comes to the new world to settle in the wilderness at the beginning of winter," he asked no one in particular. "I bet they didn't even pack a decent pair of warm socks!"

Dad obsessed over socks. One dreary winter afternoon Mom and I, out of curiosity, counted the socks in his sock drawers. We found no fewer than 137 pair, all in good shape. Dad was sore at us for doing it, and the teasing we gave him, but he insisted on putting them back himself, something about a top-secret method of organization. We never counted them again, but I suspect that by the time he passed away he was closing in on the 366 mark. Dad would have been too precise to ignore leap years.

Dad was persnickety about our vacation history lessons, too. He once corrected a re-enactor for calling a crossbow projectile an "arrow" instead of a "bolt," the proper term. He fumed that the National Gallery's description of Picasso's Blue Period was "woefully inadequate." And he was beside himself when a Colonial Williamsburg tour guide described the attire of the Williamsburg militia as "ragtag." He seemed to take personal offense that the lack of uniforms might in someway demean the skills and determination of a "group of men who could organize themselves to fight the good fight."

Over the years I got used to these moments of historical correction. My favorite was an incident at the plantation home of Thomas Jefferson: Monticello.

Our tour guide was a perky, college-aged woman with bright green eyes, curly red hair, and an endless smile. Her long, eighteenth-century dress accentuated an alluring figure. I was enchanted. But Dad ruined everything (like I, at age 13, had a shot). The problem centered on the pronunciation of "Monticello."

All through the tour, Green-eyes pronounced it "mont-a-sello," which was in vogue at the time. Every time she said it I could hear the wiring in Dad's head crackle and pop like a string of antique Christmas tree lights.

In Jefferson's bedroom, near the music stand Jefferson invented, Dad asked the guide, "Were there ever any professional musicians on the staff here at ... Monticello?" Yes, he intentionally included the home's name in his question and pronounced it "Mon-ta-chel-la."

Green-eyes made a big mistake. She corrected him, "That's a good question sir, but let's first work on your pronunciation. It's 'mont-a-sello.'"

My father was a good man. I promise. But, like Attila-the-Hun, he had his moments. This was one of them. Dad grinned and took my green-eyed infatuation to school.

"Miss," he began, "your pronunciation is an Americanized bastardization based on a misconception of what the Italian word sounds like. 'Mont-a-sello,' as you pronounce it, is wrong because 'mont' is closer to the Italian but 'sello' is an American derivative. Either we should pronounce it 'Mon-ta-chel-la', as Italian or Americanize it completely as 'mahn-ti-sello'. To pronounce a word as half-and-half is just wrong."

Green-eyes' smile disappeared. Her entire face became stern, and her reply was evasive, though not without clout. She said, "The board which oversees the house has determined that the proper pronunciation is 'Mont-a-sella.'"

Uh oh, I thought. She had just added a third pronunciation to the mix. First she said "mont-a-sellO", now she said "mont-a-sellA".

I knew Dad had caught it as well.

"Well now, which ...", he began.

He was interrupted by Mom whispering his name like a drawn-out rumble of muted thunder: – c l a r k –

There was a moment of silence. Then he said, "Never mind".

With that, green-eyes continued the tour.

Two hours later we were back in the car and headed toward the next great adventure, my mind stuck on the redheaded beauty up on the "little mountain". I felt a little bad for her and pondered her predicament.

"Dad?" I eventually offered, "too bad they didn't have tape recorders in the 1700's."

"Why's that?" He called back from the driver's seat.

"Then we'd know how Jefferson himself pronounced 'Monticello'."

I could nearly hear dad smile. "*Touché*," he said in passable French. "*Touché, Monsieur Loup.*"

Our family vacations also meant pioneer studies. By the time I was 16, I had visited more frontier homes than any message carrier for the Pony Express. These "working replicas" were generally my least favorite of our teachable pit-stops. Butter churns, oil lamps, and rickety rocking chairs are only interesting the first few times. And how many times did I watch a guide lift the corner of a bed mattress to show us that in "olden days" they did not have bedsprings. Instead they wove ropes to hold up the mattress. "These ropes would sag over time, and so the owner would re-tie them to the frames. And this is where we get the phrase 'Sleep tight' from. Isn't that interesting?"

Yawn.

The odd part is that neither Mom nor Dad seemed all that interested in these slice-of-history farms either. We seemed to be on some dreary pilgrimage to repent for the ease and comfort of modern life. On one such visit, however, Dad put on a little show that brought Mom and me to tears.

I have no memory of where this pioneer farm was, but I do recall a flat valley and blistering hot sunshine. As we walked across the grass, we created a wake in the humidity. The house was tiny and set up for self-tours. We quickly made our way through, and I think we came to the collective, though unspoken conclusion that any one of us could have written the signs. So, after our brief encounter with the 1800s, we were back outside and headed for our air-conditioned car. That's when Dad decreed we should inspect the barn.

Said barn was at least a thousand feet away, but before I could say "no", Dad was marching across the field. Mom and I surrendered and followed like a pair of POWs. We could have made a run for it, but it was too hot and we had no idea where to run.

The interior of the barn was dark and cool. Instant relief put us in a better mood. We slowly walked through and paused to chat with a pair of beautiful Belgian horses. We also gazed upon three milk cows. Everyone was avoiding the heat, and about halfway through the barn, along the south side, we came upon four white domestic turkeys resting on bales of straw.

Now it was well known that my Old Man had a

damned fine turkey call among his many vocal talents. He would start with the tip of his tongue between his lips for the initial attack of the sound and seemed to draw his tongue, and the sound, to the back of his throat during the fade out. All the while, his tongue would flap up-and-down at a rate that approximated the speed of light. Out would rush something that sounded a bit like Gahl-lah-lup-lah-lup with a French-Canadian accent.

To my classically-trained musician's ear, it sounded much closer to a real turkey than any store-bought thing I have ever heard. During the peak of his turkey-call-mastery, Dad managed to fool and confound a few mountain men, a pair of hunters, and a flock of Boy Scouts. On one of our backpacking trips in a mountain forest, Dad even managed to coerce a wild turkey to return the call.

And so, as we stood there staring at these four miserable turkeys, it was a given that he would speak to them in their native language.

Gahl-lah-lup-lah-lup? He asked. No reply.

Gahl-lah-lup-lah-lup? Still no reply.

Gahl-lah-lup-lah-lup-lah-lup-lah-lup, he encouraged.

The four turkeys were having none of this.

I admit, I felt a bit sorry for the Old Man. He looked defeated and muttered something about domestic turkeys being too stupid to understand the call of the wild. With that we turned and walked away, a cloud of dejection hanging over us. We headed toward the rear doors of the barn.

As we left, we heard human voices behind us and

glanced over our shoulders to see a young family walking into the barn at the opposite end: a mom, a dad, a little girl of about 7, and a boy of about 5. I was certainly glad they hadn't seen Dad's failed attempt at turkey chatter.

Then a miracle came to pass.

As we walked in the hot sunshine and along the outer side of the barn, we suddenly heard the little girl sing out, "Look, Daddy! Turkeys!"

That's right. As Fate or God or Beelzebub would have it, an alignment had just taken place. My family, a thin barn wall with cracks, four turkeys, and another family were destined to create a line of communication

Dad stopped.

Mom and I stopped. We knew what he was thinking.

The father in the barn said, "Yes, honey. Turkeys. Aren't they funny looking?"

"I want to hear them gobble," the little boy chimed in.

Dad licked his lips. An evil smile crept across his face. Everything suddenly got very real.

"Okay," said the clueless father in the barn, "Let's try." And with that, he merely said, "gobble-gobble" with the enthusiasm of a prostitute on a Sunday morning.

My father was a smart man. He instinctively knew that no self-respecting turkey would immediately answer. They are a rather suspicious breed of fowl, after all, so he waited – licking his lips again, preparing for the performance of his lifetime.

I transcribe thusly:

Clueless father in barn: Gobble, gobble, gobble.

    Little girl: They're not answering.

    Little boy: Try again, Daddy.

    Clueless father: Gobble, gobble, gobble.

    Dad took a breath.

    Mom: – c l a r k –

    Clueless father: Sorry kids, I guess they're not

. . .

Dad, in his Turkey Zone: **Gahl-lah-lup-lah-lup**.

    Little girl: DADDY! THEY TALKED!!

    Clueless father: Ummmm. – yeah. One did.

    Little boy: Do it again, Daddy! Do it again!

    Clueless father: Gobble? Gobble?

    Dad: **Gahl-lah-lah-lah-lup! Gahl-lah-lah-lah-lup!**

    Clueless father: Gobble gobble gobble!

    Dad: **Gahl-lah-lah-lah-lup! Gahl-lah-lah-lah-lup!**

    Kids: Laughing.

I had my hand on my mouth, trying not to laugh out loud.

    Clueless father: Gobble gobble gobble!

    Clue-searching mother in barn: Which one is it that's gobbling?

    Dad: **Gahl-lah-lah-lah-lup!**

    Clueless father: I'm not sure. It's too dark to see.

Silence. I looked at Mom. She was also about to burst out laughing. We stared at each other, sharing the mirth and the self-containment.

More silence. I imagined the turkeys sitting there

trying to figure out what the hell was going on.

Clueless father: Gobble gob . . .

Dad: **Gahl-lah-lah-lah-lup!**

Mom started biting her lower lip to stifle her laughs. I turned away because I was about to lose it just watching her.

Little girl: It's that one over there.

Clue-searching mother: Well, I just don't know . . .

Clueless father: Gobble gobble gobble!

Silence.

Clue-searching mother: You don't suppose you're getting it – umm hot?

Clueless father: It's already hot for god's sake!

Clue-searching mother: No. I mean. Like. Romantic hot . . .

Dad: **Gahl-lah-lah-lah-lup???**

Now *I* was biting my lip.

Clueless father: Gosh. I don't know. I hadn't thought of that.

Little Boy: Gobb-el. Gobb-el. Gobb-el.

Dad:**Gahl-lah-lah-lah-lah-lah-lah-lah-lah-lah-lah-lah-lah-LUP!**

Tears streamed down my cheeks. I looked over at Mom. Tears rolled down her face as well, but at the sight of my face, she had to bite her lip harder and close her eyes.

Clue-searching mother, with concern: Children. I think we should be going. I think it's time for the turkeys to nap.

Dad: **Gahl-lup?**

Clueless father: Oh Honey...

Clue-searching mother: I'm afraid one might a-t-t-a-c-k.

Little girl: Gobble gobble.

Dad: **Gahl-lah-lup ...**

Clueless father: Nah. They're harmless. See? Gobble gobble?

Dad, very loud:

GAHLLAHLAHHLAHLAHLAHALHUUUUP!

Then, dear God, in a domestic dialect, one of the *real* turkeys said, "glub-a-glub-a-glub-aglup!"

Clueless father: Your mother's right, kids. Nap-time for turkeys. Let's go.

Kids: Awwwwwww.

Real Turkey: Glub-a-glub-a-glub-aglup?

At this Dad turned around, red in the face, and trying to contain his own laughter. But he also had a serious look in his eyes.

He said, "We gotta go."

That's when I realized that the family inside was about to come OUTSIDE and see us.

Mom's eyes grew big as full moons. She let a little yip of a laugh escape. Then she turned and started walking fast. Very fast. Dad almost jogged. I simply ran.

It's not a pretty thing to see three people sitting in a stifling hot car trying to laugh and catch their breath at the same time. But it was worth it. We escaped detection. There was even something redemptive about the adventure of pranking that other family: we never stopped at a pioneer farm ever again.

PART IV
The Blues Singer

And now: here's Dr. Strange Wolfe, tickling the ivories and singing about a place that can't be found in any surveyor's field-book or map:

The West Virginia Piano Epiphany

> Paddle faster. I still hear banjos.
> –T-shirt

When I finished my master's degree in 1985, I did what most recent liberal arts graduates do. I pieced together several part-time jobs to start paying my way in the world. The core of my work package was teaching two classes for meager pay at a small college in southern West Virginia, a mountainous, coal-mining region that has produced many of the stereotypes outsiders seem to cherish about my home state. I now lived near the world of the Hatfield and McCoy feud and would soon have a moving musical adventure in those same hallowed hills.

In order to firm up my tiny bank account, I also worked three different jobs at a local music store. I gave guitar lessons, did sales on a commission-only basis, and, every once in a while, I picked up a few dollars delivering pianos. In many ways delivering pianos was the best of the three. Since ours was the only music store for over a hundred miles and since I was not insured to drive the delivery truck, I got to ride and get paid for it. Think about it: twenty minutes to load and unload the piano – total –mixed with four hours of listening to the radio and riding through some of the most beautiful spots in West Virginia. For this I would get 5 hours of minimum wage, as my manager liked me and usually rounded up my hours. The store's owner, a cocaine-addicted vet with PTSD, never caught on.

Still, when I first took the store jobs, I never expected to have a spiritual experience while delivering a spinet to an abandoned strip mine in Wild, Wonderful West Virginia. But who can know the mysterious ways of our Creator? Life lessons may come to us in the backseat of a Buick, in the growl of a hungry lion, or on a Styrofoam sign. So it was on the day of my Wurlitzer baptism.

I was on the roster to make a delivery into some of the deepest hollers of the region. Our pilot for the day was a fellow named Marcus. Marcus was the ultimate oxymoron, a quiet Marine, retired. He was shorter than me, but he had huge arm muscles, and, with a thick, bushy beard, he looked like a cross between Moses and Popeye.

As we climbed into the cab of the old moving van, I asked Marcus where we were headed. Without a word he handed me a crumpled piece of paper with our manager's miserable markings on it. By reading around a ketchup stain I deciphered the very simple directions: "US Rt. 52 West to Benchton. Stop at the diner at the curve in the road. Call the customer. He'll come get you." I should have known then we were in trouble. Most people will give you directions to their front door no matter how far out in the boonies they live. These folks didn't even try.

The drive was pleasant. Fresh spring air rushed in through my window. Some lazy, scattered clouds drifted high above the mountains, though a storm was brewing in our direction. I figured we'd beat that though – another omen ignored.

After about two hours we pulled into the parking lot of Big Ralph's Bar and Grill, "Home of the Foot Long Cheez Dawg!" That's when the sunshine began to fade.

Marcus said his longest sentence of the trip thus far, "Oh no, rednecks."

A proper translation would read, "Oh dear God in Heaven. It's a redneck bar, and we are two long-haired, bearded musicians who have to go in and ask for the freaking phone!"

Even if cell phones had existed at that time, I doubt we would have gotten a signal down in that narrow valley. Marcus and I were in a quandary.

I had been in a redneck bar only once before, and actually, it was a trailer. It was not pleasant. It was full of coal miners, loggers, and construction workers who would just as soon bounce pool balls off your Adam's apple as they would pat their girlfriends' fannies. For a while, Marcus and I just sat and watched these good ol' boys swanker into Big Ralph's for lunch and lube.

Marcus was particularly uneasy. He would stare out the windshield for a moment, then hang his head and shake it slowly back and forth. Then he would look out the windshield again hoping the bar had disappeared. He seemed to be experiencing some traumatic redneck flashback. That would be PTRD.

After a minute of this we had a polite conversation:

"Well, I'm sure not going in," I said. "They'll know I listen to Pink Floyd faster than I can dial 911."

"So," Marcus retorted. "My beard is bushier than yours!"

"My hair's longer!"

"I drove. Do I have to do everything?"

"Well, I watched for road signs."

"What signs? We've been on the same damned road for two damned hours!"

"That's right. And I verified it the whole way!"

"So?"

"So?"

So we flipped a quarter. Best two out of three.

I must say, Marcus took his loss rather well. He only dropped one F-bomb as he tried to brush his beard down with his hands. He also kept my quarter.

Finally he stepped down out of the truck and walked across the parking lot, though it wasn't really a walk. His strategy, apparently, was to try to blend in by doing the redneck strut, an indescribable bit of poetry in motion. Unfortunately, Marcus' version wasn't the least bit poetic. He had tucked his thumbs into his belt loops, which made him look more like a kangaroo attempting the Texas Two-step. Then, after about ten paces, his Marine Corps training tried to take over. The kangaroo began marching.

He fooled no one, but it was his only defense as he hop-marched into that greasy spoon.

A few minutes later Marcus came bounding out of the joint in a trot. Beads of sweat clung to his face. I reached over to put my hand on the ignition key. If an angry mob of rednecks with pitchforks came charging out, I would have fired her up to save precious time. Fortunately the crew in Ralph's decided to *stay* in Ralph's. We were in the clear.

Marcus crawled into the cab, and, I noticed, quickly locked the door.

"So, how did it go," I asked.

"It got all quiet when I went in."

"And?"

"I called the guy."

"And?"

"And we wait."

I couldn't blame him for not talking. Very few people want to discuss what it feels like to have twenty mean-spirited men size you up. You know they're thinking things like: *Why, my momma could whoop him,* or *Wouldn't it be fun to lose him in the woods near that rattlesnake den,* or the ever so popular *Too bad taxidermists won't stuff people.* All the while the theme music to *Deliverance* is buzzing in your head.

For Marcus' sake we waited in silence.

And we waited, and then waited some more. *Just how far out in the sticks do these people live,* I began I watched as the confederate flag over Ralph's began to flap in a pre-storm breeze. The sky began to turn grey.

Finally, after what seemed like an eternity on Hell's parking lot, a pick-up truck pulled up beside of us.

To this day I cannot tell you what color that truck was. It was caked in at least three layers of mud – the most recent being quite wet. Where there was no mud, there only existed rust. I wasn't sure if it was the mud or the rust that held this thing into the shape of a truck. Maybe they just clung to one another like moss on the loose bark of a dead tree.

The truck's owner was a little old man without any teeth, and he sported a week's growth of grey fur on his face. (*This guy bought a piano?*) He told us to call him "Happy," and soon we were following Happy's truck deeper into the mountains.

After we left the main highway, we followed Happy and his rust-colored, mud-trimmed Ford on a one-lane, paved road for about a mile. Then it became a gravel road. Then it became mud, as they had had a heavy rain the night before. Then the road became two, not-so-parallel, muddy ruts. We were jostled around in the cab like two peanuts caught in cotton candy machine.

When I didn't think it could get any worse, we started going up along the side of a mountain. It was a steep climb that challenged the truck considerably, tires slipping for a grip in the mud. Up and up we went, and the road did narrow. The trees also began to crowd us. Tree limbs bounced on the top of the van and scratched at the store logo on the driver's side. Once the truck even began to slide sideways.

About halfway up, the right side of the road dropped away completely, and I couldn't even see the valley floor. Worse still, we had strapped the piano to the right wall of truck. That extra weight was now on the very edge of the road. I thought we might be in the Valley of the Shadow of Death.

Then, incredibly, the road got narrow indeed.

Marcus slowed to a crawl. The left side of the van scrapped against the mountainside. I cautiously leaned forward and peered into the right-side mirror.

I nearly tossed my Oreos.

The outside dual wheel of the truck – the piano side, *MY* side – was hanging over the edge of the hollow. The inside dual, five inches of rubber on soft, muddy dirt, was all that kept us from meeting our maker. I glanced over at Marcus. He looked as sick and pale as I felt.

Finally, after about 50 feet of purgatory, the road began to widen and take on a shoulder. As we got near the mountain ridge, it opened up into a small field. But this was no ordinary patch of grass and wildflowers. It was a graveyard, a graveyard like none other I have ever seen. Most of the graves were marked with simple wooden crosses, with a few old stones scattered about, maybe a dozen graves in all. But the sign that just about did me in was a marker made from a large piece of Styrofoam. Wired to the top of it was a blue plastic, toy telephone. On the marker itself, someone had painted in crude lettering: "JESUS CALLED." The short mound of dirt and pale grass indicated the death of a child a few years ago.

I was speechless.

I can hardly remember the rest of the drive other than it seemed to go on forever. I tried to imagine who on God's green earth would decorate a child's final resting place with Styrofoam, plastic, and paint. I was repulsed by such a tacky and cheap gesture to the thievery of Death. So these were the mountains of West Virginia? Illiterate rednecks with cheese dawgs and insulting tomb–"stones." I could easily accept the wooden crosses, but Styrofoam? How could people live like that? Little did I know what was yet to come.

Happy's "house" was on top of the mountain. It was a mobile home in the remnants of a strip mine. Obviously they had pulled the house up there with a bulldozer when the road was in better shape, back when large coal trucks carried the coal down to the valley below. We were surrounded by high-walls in the nearby ridges: places where half the mountaintop was blown away to get to the coal, leaving bare, vertical rock faces, often as high as twenty feet, in the hillside. (Today, they just blast off the whole damned mountaintop.) There had been no reclamation, and the "yard" around Happy's trailer was acres of wasteland, nothing but huge briar patches and mud. The trailer itself was covered by years of dirt and mildew. A crude plywood porch had been tacked to the front. And yes, an old washing machine stood guard on the porch.

The very first thing we did with the moving van was knock down the phone line.

Oh, this day was just getting better and better.

Once the truck was positioned, we ran the ramp from the rear of the truck right onto the porch. At least we didn't have to carry the piano up the rickety steps, but we did have to unhook the washing machine and scoot it out of the way. Marcus and I then climbed into the back of the truck, unlashed the piano, and lifted it onto a dolly. That's when I heard the roar of a thousand angry elephants. It was a cloudburst. I glanced out the back of the truck and saw nothing but water. Even old Noah would have been impressed by this deluge.

Just as suddenly, Marcus and I faced a dilemma.

"Wanna take it out in this rain or wait," Marcus asked.

"I dunno. What you think?" I didn't want any responsibility for this mess.

"Do you want to slide down that road after another 2 inches of rain?"

Neither of us wanted to make a decision.

Marcus then added, "Besides, look at this trailer. Did you see that piece-of-shit couch inside? This piano'll look the same in a couple of months."

He had a point. I had seen repossessed pianos come back to the store after just three or four months. They had cigarette burns, water rings, and dirty carvings. One even came back full of beer cans. This wasn't the first time we had delivered a piano to some hicks-in-the-stix. In my mind I could see that cruddy little graveyard again.

Would I shove this piano out in the rain if it were mine? No way. But then I tried to take care of things. I wanted them to last. I would no more move my piano in the rain than I would use Styrofoam to mark the burial spot of a loved one.

"Well," Marc asked impatiently.

"Let's go," I shouted.

We tossed a moving quilt over the piano, and nearly trotted as we rolled it across the ramp. My clothes were soaked in a couple of seconds. A gust of wind whipped at the quilt like a hurricane attacking the sails of a ship. I feared lighting would strike us dead right there by the washing machine. But I lived to tell my tale (silent Marcus probably never told anyone and to this day tears up whenever he hears rain mixed with piano music).

Twenty minutes later the rain had stopped, and we were back in the truck, sliding down the mountain, and shivering in our soaked clothing. But I could not get the last scene of that darned trailer out of my head.

Happy's wife had squealed with excitement when we uncovered her new piano in the living room. She already had sheet music in her hands and was itching to get to the keyboard. While Marcus went back for the bench, I had Happy sign the paperwork. Mrs. Happy went on about how many years she had played piano for her church choir and about how she would give her grandkids piano lessons. And, sadly, I wondered if there might be one grandchild who would never know the joy of lessons with grandma.

I began to feel guilty. Deep down, I knew that the piano wasn't damaged at all. We had borrowed towels to wipe it dry, and I couldn't find any water on the soundboard. Still, guilt was there.

As Marcus and I continued our descent, fog rolled in all around us. By the time we reached the graveyard, I could barely make out the child's marker and the phone on top. I felt like an arrogant snob, and I guess I was. As we passed the last wooden cross, I had a quiet revelation. Maybe *my* values were the ones out of place. Did it matter what material was used to mark a grave? At least someone was remembered. Does it matter if a piano lasts two years or two hundred as long as it brought joy to its player? What do the numbers "2" or "200" mean in a vast universe that is billions of years old?

Albert Camus wrote that the world always conquers history in the end. He was right. There is no such thing as immortality, at least not on earth. *Nothing* lasts forever, not even the fine marble tombstones we erect to remember our loved ones. Such monuments merely give us the illusion of a final and permanent resting place. Walk through any two-hundred-year-old cemetery and see how many of those stones you can still read. By-and-by, nature simply rubs us out for good. That Styrofoam maker on a WV mountainside does not plead for immortality the way great monuments and buildings do. There was no pretension or illusion there. It *will* crumble away sooner than later.

Maybe that's the difference between Happy and me. His is another world. His home and belongings illustrate that more clearly than perhaps most of us would care to admit. He isn't out to make his name immortal; he understands the realities of life and death. While we may strive to create buildings and businesses and legacies by which to be remembered, or while we struggle with three part-time jobs to make ends meet, Happy lives for the here and now with the simple understanding that sooner or later, we will all be forgotten.

CODA

That muddy day on a mountain was nearly 35 years ago. If Happy and his wife are still alive they would have to be in their late 90s by now. I think about my misadventure with them, and Marcus, more often than I would have imagined at the time. It left a mark. I wrote the first draft of that essay just months after those events played out. Their full impact, however, has eluded me until now. My 25-year-old self waxed philosophical, quoted Camus, and expressed angry-young-man sentiments. Now that my piano moving days are well behind me (I've even sold my own piano), I see a simpler message: We humans are complex and diverse critters, and the sooner we accept that about ourselves and our differences, the sooner we can play like squirrels among the tombstones.

And in the End

When I am on my deathbed, I will ask one of my childhood friends to sit by my side. With my final gasps, I will ask him to lean in close to hear my last words. Then, just as I feel the mortal coil loosen its grip on my soul, I will slap his face silly and say, "Last Tag! You're it!"

Postface

When I was a kid, one of my favorite parts of summer vacation was staying up late every night to watch *The Tonight Show* with Johnny Carson. With two parents who were night owls, Carson was simply the perfect way for us to end those long hot days in Huntington, WV. It was our lovely habit.

The show had an organizational routine, a formula still in use on late-night TV today. Humans, I learned long ago, crave the comfort of a routine (even a bad one). And we generally love a simple routine, the simpler the better.

And *The Tonight Show* routine was bloody simple. Let me demonstrate:

PART I: The Monologue

This was our opportunity to laugh at the day's news and events, at world leaders and evil dictators, and at human stupidity and rampant cleverness. Ultimately, it was also a time for us to laugh at ourselves. The monologue might be followed by a skit or some other bit of silliness, but the purpose of Part I was simple: Get as many laughs as possible. Make us cry with laughter or do our own spit-take with our lemonade. Make us forget our worries, because at 11:30 pm, there wasn't much we could do about them anyway.

PART II: The Joke Teller

After our cares and concerns had been stuffed under our chairs and the sofa, so to speak, and after a "word from our sponsor", Carson would introduce the first guest of the evening. This was always a Hollywood A-lister or well-known celebrity. It was someone who could reel in more viewers with her or his charm and grace, and all they had to do was take a seat in the chair by Carson's desk and have a little chat with their host. We viewers were lead to believe that somehow we had scored an invite to a posh Beverly Hills party to rub elbows with the rich and famous.

Of course, it was something of an illusion. The star was in the spotlight, and they had damned well be entertaining. To that end, the most popular guests, the ones who got invited back regularly (thus helping their careers), were those who could tell a joke or two, an anecdote about themselves, maybe a bit of naughtiness, a nugget of gossip, a secret about another star – nothing too scandalous, but juicy all the same. (Robin Williams ruled this game). And, if the guest had a new movie coming out, we got to see a brief clip from the film, usually one that would make us laugh, even if the movie itself was a drama.

By the time midnight had come and gone, viewers generally found themselves in a warm-fuzzy place of contentment. They could happily march off to bed if they wanted (or needed), or they could grab one last snack during another round of commercials, and check out the next guest.

PART III: The Story Teller

The second guest was an individual of some note, but never an A-list star. They might be an up-and-coming actor, a director (Orson Wells often filled this place on the show), an athlete with a new book to pitch, a chef with a book to pitch, a politician with a book to pitch, or a photographer with a book of photographs to pitch. Upon occasion, the second guest might even be (gasp) an actual author – with a book to pitch.

These folks rarely had the pizzazz and egos of the first guest, but they often had charming thoughts to offer. Their humor might not be as over the top, but they had wit, often cracking a quip with a straight face. If the first guest was the *Yang* of the show, then the second was often the *Yin* who created a wonderful balance on the telly in the wee hours of the night.

As such, the second guest was not interested in a quick laugh; they had stories to tell, lessons to teach, and adventures to share. That's not to say the stories were without humor, but the humor in those stories was part of the fabric, the tapestry, the philosophy of a life well-lived or observed.

PART IV: The Blues Singer

As I recall, it was David Letterman who found an all-encompassing circle for this late-night formula: music. By regularly having bands and musicians on at the very end of his show, there emerged a sense of closure that set everything to rights just before we shuffled off to our bedrooms for well-earned sleep. In other words, it turns out even adults like a little music before bedtime, a lullaby – even if that "lullaby" was a hard-rocking song by Prince. By 12:30 in the morning, it didn't even matter the genre, so long as it was sincere. It could be country, rock, blues, pop, alt, or even punk. If the musician(s) gave us little words of truth with honest rhythms and melodies, we could rest our collective minds on a pillow of peacefulness. An artist could get away with singing about death as long as it dealt us a fair hand of cards to study in our dreams. (Think I'm kidding? Why the hell do we sing about babies falling out of trees to help get babies to sleep?)

One of my favorite late night TV performances is still Linda Perry and 4 Non Blondes performing their song "What's Up (What's Going On?)" on Letterman (c. 1993). I look it up on YouTube every now and again to remind myself how a powerful little anthem in difficult times can go a long way to soothe the soul, and that's really what it's all about.

Of course, now you understand the structure of this book. Shh!

Awkward Acknowledgements

Researchers tell us that men hear women's voices as though they are music. That is, when a man hears a woman speak, her voice lights up the same parts of his brain that music does.

This tells me two things:

1) Somewhere out there, there is a group of researchers with lots of free time and easy access to a CT scan machine.

2) If a woman's voice is a form of music, then a joyous female laugh is a church bell pealing in a celebration of joy.

And I believe that. I can remember the sound of a woman's laugh years after I last heard it. Which is why I, and I would suppose many other men, enjoy making a woman laugh – that and the possibility we might woo her into our beds where we ironically hope she won't laugh at us.

Making men laugh, on the other hand, offers no special rush beyond a bit of male bonding and distracting them while I cheat at poker. When I hear another man laugh, it sounds like a bit of artillery – a simple extension of the dull thud their voice makes when they talk. This is, of course, one reason I vastly prefer the company of women over men. I can hear my own voice thud and boom anytime I want.

This is not to say that the typical male laugh is useless. It just needs special accompaniment. It needs happy women. I think this is one reason men and women enjoy spending lots of money to hit a club and listen to a comic rattle off a series of one-liners: Their laughter meshes together to create even better music. Artillery as a musical instrument, you ask? Sure. Hearing a crowd of men and women laughing sounds like the bombastic ending to the *1812 Overture*! Bells and cannon fire! Glorious and triumphant!

All of which is to explain why my acknowledgments page is twisted and bipolar. I had to celebrate this observation of mine.

Here we go.

I first need to thank the women who have laughed at a few of my jokes and whose laughs I can recall in my mind as surely as the chime part to "Ring Christmas Bells." In reverse and reverent alphabetical order, because I wanna: Marlene Wolfe, Katherine Wolfe, Cynthia Dingman Titus, Melissa Shepherd, Cynthia Pinson, Lisa Palmer, Hayley Mitchell Haugen, Paula Hansford, Sandra Farrar, Beverly Delidow, and Deborah Allen.

And, thanks to a few dudes with decent artillery: Clark Wolfe, Dwayne Walters, Art Stringer, Ron Houchin, Oxford Commas, and Patrick Conner.

And finally, thank you to thousands of students and Facebook friends for your sweet laughter over these many years. It keeps me going.

Credits

In my 30+ years as a college teacher, I was late for classes a grand total of seven times. I loved teaching, and I enjoyed my students immensely. Why would I poke around getting to class? Most of the time I was 5-15 minutes early. There I would visit with students, listen to their thoughts, offer advice[1], and – entertain. Many of the jokes and such found in this book first found light in classrooms *before* classes. Many others were ad-libs and spontaneous comments. For years, I wrote these things down on notecards, cocktail napkins, and junk mail.

Then came Facebook. My mind exploded.

So it is that about 95% of the material in this collection originally found homes in those venues.

On a more formal note:

"The Seven Headless Dwarfs" first appeared in *I Must Be Off*, August 22, 2016. It still dwells on that humorous, travel e-magazine at imustbeoff.com.

"Tennyson Takes a Bullet," first appeared in *The Offbeat*, Volume 17, Spring 2017. *The Offbeat* is one of the few humor journals in the world.

---

1 [You Found It!] So the student said, "My roommate has this, this thing for girls when they puke. I mean, if it's in a movie, he'll watch it several times. And if he sees a girl puking at a party, he rushes to hold her hair for her." And I replied, "He needs to find a nice, bulimic girl." Said the young woman in the back of my classroom, "You know, there's a fetish for that."

BOOKS BY MATTHEW WOLFE
All Available at Amazon.com

Ms. Scrooge: A Christmas Ghost Story

Elvira Scrooge is a New York billionaire living alone in her Manhattan penthouse, bitter over the death of her partner, Prudence Marley. On Christmas Eve she is visited by a series of wild, modern-day ghosts hell bent on converting her from a greedy, grief-stricken sour puss into a generous and loving woman who embodies the true love that is Christmas. Based on the Dickens classic, *A Christmas Carol*, *Ms. Scrooge* mashes up original lines and language with modern day technology and life. The result is a Scrooge for the 21st century.

The Way It Was: Seven Days In The Heart Of Appalachia

Somewhere between the Hollywood stereotypes of inbred, cannibal rapists and the television image of stupid, lazy hillbillies, there are Appalachian people who are hardworking, intelligent, and beautiful. *The Way it Was* is the true story of a few of those folks. Unfortunately, that part of mountain life is disappearing in the face of the opioid crisis, suburban sprawl, and "progress."

Through a series of seven, day-in-the-life stories spread over five decades, *The Way it Was* not only illustrates the culture of southern West Virginia and its people, but it also chronicles how their unique way of life has all but died.

Wolfe was the recipient of the 2005 West Virginia Artist Fellowship in memoir writing for an early draft of *The Way it Was*.

Gentle Snow: A Gathering of Mystical Tales

Between 2004 and 2006, Matthew Wolfe felt the need, the call, to write a series of loosely connected stories about mystical people and their experiences - both real and imagined. He abandoned all his other projects and allowed these stories to come to him. This collection is a gathering of 14 of those tales. They span a time frame from prehistoric humans to the near future in a world that seems destined to destroy itself. These tales therefore ask age-old questions such as "Why are we here?" "Is there an afterlife?" "A pre-life?" "What exactly is 'God'?" And, most importantly for any mystic, indeed the very thing that defines us as mystics: "How may I touch or experience God in this world?" Gentle Snow does not attempt to directly answer those questions. Instead, the stories offer ideas and experiences that may nudge the reader to further explorations and to her or his own conclusions, even as those may change from adventure to adventure.

Gentle Snow retells the stories of venerable mystics such as Lao Tzu, Ezekiel, and Jesus. It tells the real-life stories of a woman's memories of survival and prayer during the Spanish Flu epidemic and lives devastated by a plane crash in which Wolfe tells his own story as "The Photographer." And it contains purely fictional tales of whirling dervishes, archeologists, the gates of Heaven and Hell, and reincarnation involving other realms of existence. Each of these 14 stories was written with spiritual love, and, as Wolfe describes: "They came, as best as I can tell, from the universe. I was merely the conduit, the stenographer, the translator. Writing the collection was a mystical journey, and, perhaps, it is best read that way."

HeartBeat: A Sci-Fi, Tragi-comedic, Rock 'n' Roll Fantasy Screen Book

When Ethan Blake receives a new heart harvested from a murdered FBI agent named Richard, he gets Richard's memories and mind as well. Soon they are killing Richard's killers, even as Richard's DNA assumes control over Ethan. Then with the help of Richard's lover, Karen, they uncover a deep secret: there is intelligent life beyond earth – and it is coming for us.   Based on the 2001 novel by Matthew Wolfe, the twisted ending will have you asking for more.

Note: This is a screwy script for a movie that will never get made. This is a graphic novel without graphics. This is a verbal storyboard because the author's sketches suck. This is a novel without all that intrusive detail. This is a musical fantasy. Buckle up your harshest rocker voice to sing through the scenes. This is a dramedy. You'll laugh. You'll cry. You may wish for the writer's death.

www.ingramcontent.com/pod-product-compliance
Lightning Source LLC
Chambersburg PA
CBHW071537040426
42452CB00008B/1045